By turning this page you agree to join

THE LONE WRITER'S

low-stress
high-reward
eminently-portable

WRITING CLUB

March 16, 2016

Esteemed Lone Writer,

Every week my writer friends and I try to meet and write together. If we're in town and have time we meet in person, but usually we meet by phone. In the early days just one of us offered a prompt or theme to write about that day. Later, it morphed into each of us offering a prompt so we'd have a choice. Some of us even tried to include all the prompts in our response. Each time we meet we say hello, talk about the weather, then give the prompts, hang up and write. Twenty minutes later we call back and read what we've written to one another. After a year of doing this I realized how much better I liked my writing when I didn't have time to think about it. I found my pieces had more sparkle despite errors in grammar or spelling, despite meandering thoughts or confused ideas. In fact, I think the sparkle was due to those idiosyncrasies. There was always something that surprised me or caused me to think I'd like to write more about whatever had surfaced.

A prompt can be anything. Sometimes it's a poem or part of an essay. Sometimes it's as simple as the words 'Kindergarten' or 'Swimming Lessons.' The feedback we give each other might be I sure want to know more about that! or, I got lost when you said that thing about your uncle. Because we do this almost every week, and because I've grown to love and trust my writing friends, I've learned to enjoy and trust my own writing, too

Writers often tell me they wish they had a writing group like ours. My hope is that the prompts and stories in this book will inspire you to write as though you have a group. Scribble your thoughts in the margins, fill up extra pages, edit what these writers have written, write the first story that comes to mind when you see the prompt. Don't think too much. Go on tangents. Write without editing. Edits and re-writes come later. And if you can't think of something to write, make something up.

Enjoy yourself. Write what's true.

Bar

How to use this book:

Each prompt is printed at the top of an empty page so you have room to write your response. Limit your self to seven minutes, ten minutes, or twenty at the most. Set a timer and stop when it beeps. After you're done, read my friends' responses. Some are more polished than others. Some wander. Some are literal and some are metaphoric. Some hardly make reference to the prompt. At the end of each of their responses is another prompt, but ignore those if something else is more compelling for you to write. Always write what you're on fire about. If you don't feel like writing something it'll sound like that when you're done. If you're stuck, write about being stuck. If you can't think of anything to write, write about not being able to write. And if you're in the middle of writing and your thoughts take some goofy turn, follow them. Have lots of extra paper on hand.

My only request is that you write for us. I've put our pictures on your empty pages to remind you to do that. In other words, see how it feels to write for others VS how it feels to write in your journal. If you're a fiction writer, write from your characters' points of view. Get to know them. Give us all the details you can. What does the kitchen smell like? What fabric was on the couch? What was your heart really doing when someone you loved left you? Remember that we know nothing about you, your characters or the story you want to tell, so fill us in! Tell us as much as you can. And if you're worried that someone else might not like what you write, or that someone might read what you've written when you're not around to stop them, keep this book with you. Hide it in your glove compartment, put it in your t-shirt drawer. Many of us worry about what others will think. This book is a place to forget all those others (except for us!)

bar   annie   tilly   michelle   penny   doris   charlotte   janet   debra

Here's your first prompt:
Draw a picture of yourself and / or your characters

Here's your second prompt:

Kindergarten

Mrs. Fenner said "who has that beautiful voice?" as she strode behind me one of those first warm days when I was five years old and so shy, so very shy.

We were singing this old man with Mrs. Dolan at the piano as our accompanist, banging on the black and white keys, her white short bob following the leaning in and out of her head as she felt the music she played, her black sturdy shoes sliding back and forth between foot pedals, me tugging at my dress, attire I wasn't used to wearing.

As soon as Mrs. Fenner said those encouraging words, I clammed up, couldn't sing, couldn't speak, I hung my head, wanting to disappear, and she seemed to know me, seemed to have a sense of this awkward bird in her classroom, so she placed a hand on the back of my shoulders, lightly, warm, smelling of chalk and faint perfume, her heavy body wrapped in a nondescript dress, her hair in a long single braid that was trussed up over and over around her head, she touched my shoulder, my back, my neck and though I never said or sang another word, my heart was filled with hope.

Which one of your teachers stopped you in your tracks?

Our kindergarten picture says it all: Walter Burrows, John Walters, Nancy Brown sitting there with the rest of us: Laurie Inglish, Cathy Giles, Victor Williams, me. Integration. We didn't even understand the word. Walter, John, and Nancy were our friends. We didn't play at their houses after school but that's because their houses weren't in our neighborhoods. They took the bus just like we did. It's just that their journey was longer. I hadn't thought of that until just now. It wasn't until after we graduated from college that I went to Nancy's house, and even then, I only stuck my head in the door. By then, I lived down the street. My first apartment was on the same block. Nancy lived with her mom. No dad in sight. I never knew where John or Walter lived. Somewhere in that neighborhood for sure. That's where all the black kids lived. Their houses were small and generally not maintained. Or was it just that they were poor. Now those houses are the houses up-and-comings buy to wiggle their way into suburban Philadelphia life. Nancy lives in Wayne now. She's a single mom too. Loves Jesus and says so regularly on Facebook. John lives in Erie, Pennsylvania. He teaches at a boy's choir school out there. Don't remember the name. He and Nancy and I sang together all through high school. We fashioned ourselves after Lambert, Hendrix and Ross, the famous trio by that name. The original group was one of the first integrated singing groups. One black man (Hendrix) a white woman (Ross) and a white man (Lambert). Scandalous, but I'm not sure we even knew about that when the three of us sang together. We were protected from a lot of things in the early 1960s. The three of us recorded a few Christmas songs together after we graduated from college. It was the second time I'd done a recording session and I felt as though my life was truly beginning; that the whole world was opening up to me. Nancy brought that project to my attention this past winter wondering if I still had a copy of what we sang. I don't and wish I did. I remember making my family sit in my brother's room on Christmas morning that year so that they would listen to the songs. I didn't want to play them while mom was cooking or when everyone else was distracted by presents. I wanted them to hear every word. I'm still like that: I want people to sit and listen the way they would pay attention to a movie or a poem. But people don't feel that way about songs. They'll sit and listen to a symphony or an opera -- the classical forms – but pop songs like mine are meant for background listening. They set a mood while people are doing something else. I wonder how I could change that? I wonder how I could cause people to listen more closely to all the music they love.

What did you do in the talent show? How'd it go?

(you'll need extra paper here. There's some in the back of the book)

I don't think that I was particularly sophisticated at five-years-of-age. I wasn't watching Downton Abbey nor was I part of a cocktail circuit that involved mixed drinks. I didn't know about cleavage or high heels. I didn't know about fine food or fast cars. Under the watchful eye of my grandparents living downstairs and my parents living above them upstairs, I was sheltered. Aside from overhearing adults whispering cautions to one another, such as "Little pictures have small ears," I didn't know much outside the confines of home.

And yet I had aspirations. I can't tell you what they were, but like a dog that aspires to run free or a cat that aspires to lie close to the woodstove, I dreamed of bigger things – bigger things than running out in the street to buy fruits and vegetables from the blind man who peddled produce from his wooden wagon drawn by a moth-eaten horse. Or maybe the blind man could see a little – but at five, it was so much more exciting to imagine that he was totally blind.

Given my yearning for life outside the confines of my street and family, you would suppose that I would have looked forward to starting kindergarten. My kindergarten class photo shows me sitting in the front row. I am wearing brown, tie-up Buster Browns, white ankle socks, and a plaid dress with a white, Peter Pan collar. My blond hair is chin-length. My bangs are uneven. I do not look very self-confident or dreamy.

Mom had set a bleak tone. Walking to school that very first day, my mother confided that I had been assigned to the very same teacher whom she had had. The teacher was frightful. So frightful that Mom admitted to being afraid to enter the classroom with me for fear that the teacher would recognize her as a former pupil.

This was not a good beginning.

Twice a week we had music. Rhythm was an important part of the music curriculum. Week after week the teacher gave me two, dowel-like sticks. No drum accompanied the sticks. Was it my bad haircut? Maybe my dress? Maybe my mother? I aspired to play the tambourine. But week after week, the tambourine rotated between the other children.

They say "the sins of the parent are visited on the child." Did I put the teacher off or did the teacher remember my mother?

My next birthday, I'm going to buy a tambourine. It is not too late.

What do you still want for your birthday?

Before we heard the next prompt, Charlotte read the poem "Claim" by Jasey Jueds, about a dog that leads the way.

From Keeper ©2013 *University of Pittsburgh Press*

Who rescued you?

How were you rescued?

I think of all the dogs who've rescued me in one way or another: Mea, MaGirlMaGirl, Henry the Dog, MaceyG, and Foofoomoo. But Silver, that exquisite Doberman I adopted when I was 22, was my dog. The others came with husbands. Silver was the one who leaned his heavy black butt on my lap whenever I sat on the couch, the one who let me wrap him in a blanket as he fell into the space under my desk, the one who let me use him as a pillow when we lay on the cushy bench in the kitchen. Other people were afraid of him. He was big and boxy, and his tail and ears had been cut to meet the standard of champions; cut before he was old enough to object.

In New York City, when we walked down 8th Avenue to Central Park, passersby would get out of our way, cross the street if they were really afraid. They didn't know his gentleness. After a walk in Central park at dusk one night, he strutted down Broadway with a limb he'd found that was as long as the sidewalk was wide. So proud he was! He strutted like a thoroughbred that's won the Kentucky Derby. Like a king who's won an important victory. On-lookers laughed and smiled as we passed – him on a leash, me, his follower.

We danced together once in the Park. It was early on a Saturday morning in a place where dogs were free to run. No one else was there at first. Our private hill overlooked the lake where later in the day lovers would rent rowboats and move slowly, romantically across the water.

I was a dancer that morning. Who knows what propelled me. I turned, spun, revolved, around and around. Silver was my lover. He didn't bark. He didn't jump around demanding my attention. He too spun and ran in gentle circles on the hill. Both of us off lead. Both of us moving with grace and care-less-ness. Both of us aware of the photographer taking pictures of us from below. Photos we have never seen. Photos that caught it all.

When did you do something that someone else watched and enjoyed?

If you are rescued is it the same as being saved? If it's different, why is it different and how do you, the person rescued or saved, actually know?

In the mirror I see dark eyes, more brown than I remember. I see eyebrows arched naturally no plucking maintenance needed. I see a nose wide like my father's, but different from the wide nose of my husband, my daughters. In the mirror, I see the powder falling from my nose resting just above the top of my lip. I see the powder and feel my hand come up to wipe it away, to adhere it to my finger and then swiftly to my tongue before the crystals disintegrate.

I see my life and become aware that I am trapped. Trapped inside the darkness that fills the eyes looking back at me. I see and do not believe.

Beside the mirror is the only door, the only exit from a bathroom almost too small for me and it is moving just a little bit toward me.

"Wait!" I see my lips moving in the mirror.

"Wait" I say again as my lips move in the mirror.

"Mommy!" Her words are urgent. Her dark and almond shaped eyes are likely filling with tears, but my foot is firmly against the door.

"Mommy!" She cries now, reaching the door knob, rattling it to open it.

In the mirror I see dark eyes framed by arched brows. I see my hand wipe away the powder, touch water to my nose, clear the crystals from my lip.

I hear her body slide down outside the door, know the tears fall freely down her face as she begs, "Come out!"

I don't know if I was rescued or saved. I don't know if there's a difference or even if there needs to be. But if I were asked, "Who rescued you?" My answer would always be she did.

Look in the mirror. What do you see?

Look Out The Window. Describe What You See?

The porch swing hangs empty waiting for the warmth of the rising sun to seep through the Cedars. A farmer's feed pan sits atop an up-ended log. A Crested nuthatch flies to the shag. Hops closer… and closer yet…and finally hops to the edge of the pan to look for bird food. He doesn't stay long. The Pinon jays have beaten him to the bounty. It is slim pickin's.

A rock perimeter surrounds the neglected garden. Two, dead, cedar shags stand sentinel – landing pads for in-coming birds who want to take advantage of the seeds and bird bath. Three, large, variegated green and white agaves grow at the base of the shags. But otherwise, you might say that the garden, devoid of flowers, has gone-to-seed.

At ground level, an in-ground, cement birdbath holds water which is dark olive and opaque glassy white – a trick of shadow. Next to the birdbath and in the shadow of the shag and agave, lies a bronze-colored statue of a young nymph. She lies on her stomach – knees bent, feet in the air, ankles crossed. She has propped herself up on her elbows and in her hands she holds a book.

I love this girl – living in the dirt under a cactus – reading of far off places. Maybe she is reading about walking a forest path or wading in the surf… oh look! A Sandpiper!

A rabbit approaches the garden and tentatively hops six inches and then takes another cautious move – another six inches. It is a slow process. The rabbit stops to listen. He finally makes it to the edge of the sunken birdbath, cocks his head for one more listen and then heedless of danger, dips his head to drink. He drinks thirstily as if he has not drunk in a long time.

A half mile away, the traffic on Highway 50 hums.

Where were you when you saw **The Birds?** *Haven't seen it yet? How 'bout a movie you saw at the Drive-in?*

The courtyard is overgrown. Four pine trees envelope it. They're not yet golden, but many of their leaves are already on the ground. Winter is on its way. I see that Mea pooped out there last night so she must have really had to go despite my having walked her a few minutes earlier. She never poops in the courtyard. I'll clean it up later. Thankfully it's a nice sturdy poop. Easy to pick up. I never planted my flowerpots this year. There didn't seem to be a point. I say I'm going to sit out there each morning and read or write. Michael dreams about late night glasses of wine by the chiminea, but that never happened. The summer has gone by and we haven't enjoyed time at all. We've been racing against the clock for months now. It makes me wonder why we live here if we aren't going to slow down to the tempo of rural life.

The windows were my idea and I insisted. They're big, well-built and well insulated. They turn out on a 45-degree angle for just enough air to come through in winter, but not so much that the wind will rip them off in summer. Anderson. I love their windows. I like when I have the good sense to do things right. Before we changed them out, they were short and high on the wall. The room was like a dungeon despite its east-facing wall. This morning the 3-foot long windows are filled with the patchy morning sun coming through the leaves. The cobwebs I swore I wouldn't let build up, have done just that. The screens have dings from the contractor's sloppiness installing them - nothing to complain about, just enough to wish he had been more careful at the time.

Hal and Jamie are leaving this morning. I wonder if they'll ever be back. We're at the age now when you never know if the person you're saying good-bye to will be back. There's no reason to think one of them will go to the heavens any time soon, but we are that age. Maybe it'll be one of us. Who knows. I wish I could live each day as though it were my last like the self-help books suggest. I could only do that when Theo was sick, and even then it was hard. After all it wasn't me who was dying.

Michael is leaving today too. Maybe while he's gone I *will* sit out in the courtyard. Last week I couldn't wait for the time alone. This week, I'm lonely and he hasn't left yet. I think about his death all the time. All the time.

Was there a time when you bought something big that you couldn't afford?

For years, in my 20s and 30s, I lived on my own / except when I was living with a man I loved / in a few different places. When I was living on my own, it came from wanting to get away from someone or some living situation that felt restrictive or unhappy or some combination of those.

My first time living on my own happened because I had fallen in love with a man that one of my housemates didn't approve of me seeing. She thought he was too young and spread an aura of judgment to encircle me.

I moved into a tiny cottage to escape her prying.

This cottage was near a lake and it was never constructed to be lived in year 'round – poorly insulated and drafty, pipes that were vulnerable to freezing in the harsh winter temperatures, one propane heater to huddle around when the cold winds rustled the curtains inside the dark living room.

The cottage was just a living room, bedroom, another room, a rectangular kitchen and a bathroom that also served as a closet for the hot water heater. All the rooms were small. Cheap, dark wood paneling. Mildew that crept up the closet walls and ruined several pairs of my shoes and boots before I discovered it. Indoor / outdoor carpeting. Chipping linoleum.

I loved that cottage. It represented freedom to me. The bedroom was sunny. I fixed the place up as best as I could on my own with little income.

My mother gave me the Farberware percolator that had been one of their wedding presents 20-some years before – it was exactly my age – and I still use the same type coffeemaker today because, even now, once in a while, the aroma and sound of percolating coffee on a winter morning takes me back to that tiny cottage and the joy I felt living there.

The young man I loved could come over and we could spend time together without my feeling the weight of my friend's piercing looks. I had small dinner parties and took walks to the lake and felt so independent and grown up.

The kitchen walls were sunny yellow and it was my first of many cozy homes. I think I only lived there about a year – so long ago now, I can't be sure – but I loved that place and that man. So much.

A cabin, a lake, and a hardware store. Ring a bell?

My first apartment was on County Road in Ardmore on the edge of the Black neighborhood. Behind my building were Italians; in front, the Black kids I've only recently figured out were bussed to four different elementary schools when we were all kids in the '60s. Nancy Brown and her mother were four doors down. Both were large, fleshy women; the kind of women you merge with when you hug them. Nancy and I sang together in the choir and later in smaller ensembles with John Burrows who lived two doors down from her. We were the Mod Squad for a while. Now we're friends on Facebook. She's a single mom now too. John's an actor living in Erie, Pennsylvania doing musical theater.

Our apartment stretched the length of the first floor of the narrow single-family home turned multi-dwelling complex. It was a broken down building with a rickety back entrance through an aluminum screen door, and a more substantial but poorly maintained wooden front door. I rented the enclosed front porch from the woman who had the lease. She had the big bedroom at the back. The kitchen had no cabinets, a freestanding old fridge and a brown linoleum floor. The only bathroom was small and grungy, just off the kitchen. Between my 10'x 10' porch and the kitchen was a dining room, a sitting area, and my closet.

The woman I rented from, whose name I've forgotten, must have had money in her past. Her rugs and furniture were elegant and formal. They didn't belong in this space. I didn't know her. I'd answered an ad in the paper a few months after graduating from college when it was time for me to get my own place. I was money to her. Neither of us was interested in friendship or conversation. We avoided one another as much as possible. She and her boyfriend – probably a married man given their odd and frequent meeting times – had loud and, I thought, too aggressive sex I couldn't avoid over-hearing. I worried about her at times but she always seemed pleased when I'd see her in her robe a few hours later. Her cats ate the wires to my stereo speakers. That's when I moved out. It was not a happy time but it was my first step into my own life, away from the comfy home I'd grown up in.

I loved my little room there. I got my first piano there – an upright that I scraped and re-finished until it looked pretty good and sounded ok, too. It was the room where I set-up my first four-track recorder and removed myself from the world with headphones. I wrote my first real song there: "Friday Night," a quirky song, half spoken half sung, about a shy high school girl going to her first dance in the school gym. That room is where I closed the doors and cried when John Lennon was shot, and it was the room I was in when I fell for Jim, the man who encouraged me to write songs, who taught me about my creativity, and who later wrecked my heart by denying me.

When did an animal wreck something of yours?

What were you denied?

Warning Signs

When I Said Too Much

Money as Therapy

Before we got the following prompt, Penny read from Annie Dillard's book The Writing Life, *where the author talks about how a work in progress is feral, wild, and needs to be tamed like a mustang, that this can only done by visiting everyday and reasserting your power over it. The passage was from chapter three.*

When Your Writing is Feral

I was reading in bed when Keith came in. I don't know how her name came up, if I was having lunch with her the next day or if she was coming over to our house so I could give her a Reiki session, but I remember my husband asking, "You know she's in love with you, right?"

Without even looking up from the book, I said, "You always say that, but I think what you're picking up on is my body reacts when I'm around her."

I said it matter-of-factly. I said it without looking up from the page, but when I did, his face told me I had said too much. His eyes were wide, his face troubled. He tightened the belt on his bathrobe. Even though I had said too much he wanted to know more.

"What do you mean your body reacts? You're attracted to her?"

"No, I'm not attracted to her—she's pretty, but that's not what I mean. I mean my body reacts…"

"So you're attracted to her…," he said.

We got tangled up in semantics. What I was trying to say was I didn't want to sleep with her. I didn't want to be with her and not him. But it was undeniable: When she was around, my stomach dipped. I pulsed. I felt awkward and nervous, like a teenager at a school dance. When she was around, I peeked at her cleavage and followed the curve of her muscular arms and back.

We met while I was out walking the dogs, the day before I was to have bunion surgery on my left foot on Halloween 2007. She was driving through our little town in a brand new metallic green Jeep Wrangler that said both "I'm cool" and "I have money." She pulled over, leaned out the window while her boys popped up out of the open top.

"Beautiful dogs," she said. Her long, light brown hair hung below a hip headband. She wore sunglasses.

"Thank you," I said.

"Can we pet them?" the boys pleaded. They were maybe 4 and 8. One was towheaded like my son was at his age; the other skinny with brown hair.

"No, not today," she told them.

"Mom!" they groaned.

"We have to get home for supper," she said.

We swapped a few more pleasantries. When she drove away, I wished I had gotten her name, but it was a small town, so I knew I'd see them again.

Months passed. I had my bunion surgery, which kept me on crunches for three months, and then it was another four months before I really got out and started walking again. I was overweight after lying around for months after my surgery. By the time spring rolled around I was anxious to get back outside and to get the weight off. I had also decided to take Pilates—an exercise that had helped me tighten and firm when I did it years before.

One day while waiting in line at a coffee shop, a business card seemed to call out to me. I took one from a stack and was surprised to see that it was for a Pilates center I had never heard of before. I emailed the woman later that day and she wrote back a very friendly response. We exchanged emails and I tried to figure out how to get $150 for three private sessions.

I was out walking the dogs, plotting how I would drop the weight by my birthday in May, when I saw the green Jeep again. The woman pulled over and the boys popped up again and we continued our conversation from the past fall. This time I was determined to not let her get away without knowing her name.

"By the way, I'm Ann. I live over on Meadow Lane," I said, extending my hand to her.

"Melissa," she said. "Melissa Donovan." Excitement shot through me: She was the woman I had been exchanging emails with about Pilates. It was a sign—I knew it, she knew it.

Somehow I would find the money to work with her. I had to.

When did you find money you didn't think you had?

None of these prompts work for me today, at least not immediately. I don't feel like writing the obvious for 'Warning Signs': Ben wanting Sarah to be at our wedding, Ben calling Sarah repeatedly on the sly, my catching him repeatedly when I didn't mean to and didn't want to, or Ben sleepless and distracted when Sarah was in danger. I'm tired of them and I'm bored with writing about it.

'Saying Too Much' is a curse I'm blessed and burdened with. I often talk too much, say too much, blurt things out that I think will be funny but aren't. There are hundreds if not thousands of examples – so many that I can't even think of one. Trying to conjure one up to write about makes my eyes cross behind my skull. Yet I write memoir. I encourage myself and others to "go deeper," "tell us more," "give us the juicy bits," not for the shock value but for the value of truth telling. When I read memoir that withholds a detail or a character flaw, I can feel it and I get bored. When a writer insists that her main character is always happy she's not a believable writer. There are probably those who have that view of my writing – or worse: me!

'Money for Therapy' in one of my themes. Less so now than when I was young: I bought things to prop myself up, make myself look good. I think of expensive devices I bought that were more than I needed but had some cache. But like the other prompts, this is a subject I'm bored with. The prompt itself came from a self-help book our therapist suggested called *Money Therapy*. It's lying on the floor at my feet. I read it every so often to knock some sense into myself. On the cover I've put a Post It note that says, "Budgeting does not equal deprivation." Carl, our therapist, wants me to think about my belief that if I make a monthly budget I won't have what I want. I'm not a realist when it comes to money. I've always believed, and it's mostly been true, that everything works out. Bills get paid. Every time I pull my credit card through a keypad I'm pretty much relying on that belief. So boring.

And Annie Dillard? She's in the same category as Bob Dylan for me: I don't get it. Annie's sentences are too formal, too well written, so dense with meaning and self-worthiness that I tune her out then feel smug *and* inferior. Bob Dylan? I know his lyrics are supposed to be brilliant, but I don't understand them. When I hear others sing them it's better, but I always feel like my suburban Philadelphia upbringing has insulated me from feeling the cultural pain that he describes. And I can't tolerate his voice. Generally I love non-singers like him. Singers who, in my view, are the greatest singers: Randy Newman, Tom Waits, Rickie Lee Jones. These people whose voices aren't smooth, they're raspier like speech, they have a need to sing that I can feel. I've never heard that in Dylan's voice. When I hear him sing it's like I'm resisting being shaped by a metal file. Harsh words that feel like sacrilege to write. I can even feel my heart racing and my underarms getting moist knowing I'll have to read this aloud. Someday maybe I'll understand them both.

When did you buy something to make yourself feel better? Did it work?

Who do you dislike that everyone around you seems to love?

It was the look on her face coupled with the sound of her voice, a rising questioning tone that caused me to move to the right lane, slowing in traffic as we headed down the highway. We'd taken a short break from the routine of our lives to sit by the ocean, listening as waves lapped the sand it hugged and the sand surrendered and let go. Sharing that sense of how big and small we are in the world. She couldn't have been more surprised as I chattered on telling stories of my life.

The two-lane road away from one beach town and on the way to another suddenly seemed a metaphor I couldn't quite grasp. I could see the subtext in the lanes, but found I wasn't sure what it all meant. Something I couldn't quite understand just passed by in our conversation.

After a few minutes of dissipating traffic, I chanced a look over for clarification. Breathing out a "What?", my heart beat rapid and strong. Her gaze steady through the windshield felt less passenger-side riding and more driving with determination. There was definitely something.

"I didn't know that." There, she'd said it. Relayed the message clear and with the resilience of high definition radio. The pin dropped and the message rose swiftly to the top and there it was.

Oh shit, I done said too much.

When did you realize it wasn't going to work?

It is hard to imagine Annie Dillard's work becoming feral, but I certainly identify with the intention of the quote. I have hyphenated a-work-in progress because the work is linked to progress and yet…"the work" itself is solid, but the progress is ephemeral – progress is early morning mist on the mountains: the sun warms, and the mist dissipates; progress is storm clouds building on the horizon that fail to deliver; progress is…

Writing of my own work, some work is already written but some thoughts on work are only brief flashes that light the sky and disappear before I can catch them. I find that progress is exceedingly slow. I am so easily distracted by an unwashed dish, an unmade bed, an unwatered garden, an unanswered letter, an unpaid bill. And as I write this, I notice all of my adjectives start with the prefix "un."

And that "un" says it all. "Un is a vacuum – a negative space that begs to be filled. Which leads me back to my lack of self-discipline.

I like to imagine myself in a convent. The windows are narrow slits. The doors are locked. The bed is hard and the covers inadequate. The floor is stone. I am cold. I can't get warm. Visitors are admitted but a grilled separates us. meals would be prepared. Meditation would be required. Silence would reign. Mother Superior would stand ready with a switch. Not that her birch switch would hurt me, but the notion of being switched – not by my own mother, but by another adult would be humiliating. This fear of humiliation would keep me at my desk.

Writing would be my only outlet. I would be inspired and productive. I would make progress.

What have you left undone?

Rules

The Space Between Us

Time you enjoy wasting is not wasted time

This is the world. Beautiful and Terrible Things Will Happen. Don't be Afraid.

You don't call or write anymore. I can feel you pulling away. What did I do to make you want to leave me? I did not ask for this. Are you happy? Content? Do you feel lighter without me? How does it feel to be single again?

Do I really want you back? "What part of you do I miss the most," I ask myself.

I miss the security knowing that I have someone to come home to each evening. I miss hearing about your day. I miss having someone to take care of.

I've got all this time on my hands. Were you really the perfect mate for me? When I look back, I don't think you could fully receive my love. I think we did the best we could with what we knew. We worked extremely hard and built a home together, but we didn't really play. You couldn't let go and just laugh and have a great time.

You found happiness at the beach, on your bike, or on a run. Your world was so insular. You worked a lot. We never took any road trips. I had to arrange all the fun activities. You were only fully relaxed when we left town and went on vacation.

Why do I want you back so badly? Why do I miss you? Do I really miss *you*? What is it that I truly miss? Was I just married in name only? Maybe I crave having a companion, a playmate. I don't know. In the meantime, I miss you. A lot. Now there's just a space between us.

How old were you the first time your heart was broken?

How 'bout the second time?

I'd forgotten about that feeling. Stretching my inner thighs, my outer thighs, my neck, back, and arms. When I first sat down, I thought *here I am in the sun with ten minutes. I could read. I could write. I could knock on the door and go in.* The sun felt warm, warm enough to remove my jacket. Ants crawled across the pavement causing me to rethink the option of lying flat on the driveway. I'm not afraid of ants, I just don't like the feel of them crawling on my skin or up my pants. I thought *well, I could just sit here. Do nothing. I haven't done nothing for a long time. Surely nothing would be a good thing for me to do.* But hard. So I stood, remembering that a few extra minutes is a good time to stretch particularly when the sun is out. Arms to the sky thinking about the vultures in the tree above me who were up there yesterday too. Wings stretched in flight or to dry after a moist morning. Then down, slowly, down to the ground, feeling a slight twinge, reminding me not to push, to breathe, to sigh. Leslie taught me to sigh. In any position when the stretch feels tight, at the very end, sigh. The sound, the act of sighing releases the muscles just a little bit further. That sigh got me in trouble once. Not trouble really, just confusion for my dear, 93-year-old father. I had decided to stretch in the bathroom on the 2nd floor. It's the only room in their house with a door and enough floor space for a person to lie down in private. So I was there on the rug, twisting on my back, pulling my bent knees from side to side, slowly, rhythmically, sighing repeatedly, on the floor for several minutes. My father – in his office right next door, overhearing this rhythm, these sighs, not understanding – finally said, "I think it's time for you to come out of there, Charlotte." *Why?* I thought surprised because I was in the quiet zone. It didn't occur to me until a few minutes later what he'd been thinking. Too late to say "I was stretching, Dad" just so he wouldn't think ill of me. Does he think I would spend so much time in his house enjoying myself in such a way with or without him nearby? I wonder. But it was too late to explain. If I'd tried, he and I both would have had to acknowledge what he was thinking and I couldn't bear that. Wouldn't do that to my dad.

What did you do that your parents misunderstood? Would they understand if you explained it?

The space between us pulsates, vibrates. It pulls us in and confuses us. I'm married. You're not. Still, we won't cross that line. We will leave with our integrity intact. Coming together under the covers isn't necessary because the connection is far deeper than that. I don't need to lie next to you, naked, but oh my, do I want to feel your skin, touch your breasts, kiss you long and deep.

I have to go home, back to him, back to the life I've created in Iowa. But this space between us will not widen. It will gather into itself. It will stitch us together even though we are hundreds of miles apart, even though I am white, a Midwesterner, blonde, blue-eyed—no one you have ever considered for yourself. You're black, a New Yorker who can't fathom how we will ever be more than distant friends.

That space between us doesn't stay intact. It can't. A force we don't comprehend is pulling us together. The space between us disappears through phone calls and emails, G-chats and hotel rooms.

I leave him—not for you, no, but for me. I move farther away from you so that I can be closer to me.

I leave but in the going, I take you along. In my heart. In the space between us.

What did you leave behind?

It is late, and I am on the bus headed north up to Green Lanes. The bus is nearly empty. A young couple furtively gropes one another in the back of the bus. A middle-aged woman with impossible red hair sits up front. A woman with silver, sequined shoes worn with sock sits across the aisle. And that's it. As I said, the bus was nearly empty.

The bus stops, and an elderly man comes on. He swipes his Freedom Pass and starts down the aisle There are lots of empty seats. I'm sitting half way down the bus on the right. The driver steps on the gas, and the elderly man lurches forward.

He wears a Russian-like cap with built in earflaps, a plaid muffler, a greatcoat, and more. I can't see beneath his coat, but it is obvious that he is dressed in layer after layer. Maybe he is wearing everything he owns.

Hanging on to the backs of the seats for balance, he works his way down the aisle, and when he reaches my seat, he stops and falls in beside me. Of all the empty seats, why mine?

He speaks to me in a heavy foreign accent. Who am I? Where am I from? Where am I going? To each question I give a brief answer. Meanwhile, he is moving incrementally closer and closer yet. First we are just joined at the hip. Later at the shoulder.

Like an animal, he burrows in. I am not a woman. He is not a man. I am merely a warm place. I hope our mute communion warms him as much as it warms me.

Have you ever met someone you'd like to meet again?

Your First Favorite Song

A Lie in the Service of Truth

The first song I memorized was "Joy to the World" by Three Dog Night. I thought my sister would think I was cool if I could sing along with them. Not so much. **What did you do to try to impress someone else that didn't work?**

Way, way back, what I first remember is the feeling. The feeling of knowing a tune so well it sings itself in my head and taps itself in my footsteps. The words tumble over and over in my mouth. I remember the feeling of a favorite song before I remember the song.

According to the baby book my mother kept for me, the song I loved to sing as a toddler was "The B-I-B-L-E."

The B-I-B-L-E/ Yes! That's the book for me./ I stand alone on the word of God,/the B-I-B-L-E

It has a bouncy little tune, so I can imagine it was fun to sing. But who knows if it actually was my favorite, or if my mom just wanted it to be.

Of course, the songs that get stuck in our heads are not always favorite songs. Sometimes they're just stuck. A friend of mine calls this song bondage.

But the first song I remember discovering on my own -- the first song I remember having power over me -- was from the Barbra Streisand movie, *Yentl*. It is the story of a Jewish woman who feels God made her to study the Bible at a time when her tradition only gave this privilege to men.

Something in the combination of story and voice, lyric and melody ignited in my own life. It spoke for something in my 12-year-old experience that nothing else in my world had been able to say. The song was "Piece of Sky."

It all began the day I found/ that from my window I could only see a piece of sky
I stepped outside and looked around/ I never dreamed it was so wide or even half as high!
The time had come to try my wings/ and even though it seemed at any moment I could fall
I felt the most amazing things,/ things you can't imagine if you've never flown at all...

The orchestration, Barbra Streisand's powerhouse voice, the look on her face in the movie as she sang. All of this unlocked something achy and hungry in me. Something desperate but also vague. Something I still can't name without diminishing it.

The way I heard them, the final lines of the song stood bravely against the small space of small-minded tradition. They leaned into a divine call toward God's inherent gift of something bigger and vastly more beautiful. All of it wrapped in the rapturous emotion only an adolescent heart can feel.

What's wrong with wanting more?/ If you can fly, then soar.
With all there is, why settle for just a piece of sky?

I begged my mother to buy the record of the soundtrack for me. I played it over and over until I knew it by heart.

Where was the stereo in your house? Who got to use it?

Was it a lie or was it withholding? I don't know if it makes a difference. Either way I didn't do what I was supposed to do. Looking back, I don't know how I could have done things differently, but of course I could have. I could have blurted out the whole beautiful truth and it would have hurt people just as thoroughly. The advantage would have been that I'd know I hadn't lied, hadn't withheld, that I'd done what I needed to do for myself.

I'm talking about falling in love, that wonderful feeling I hadn't felt in over fifteen years. My skin hot and damp to touch, my heart beating hard enough that I could feel it in my chest, and my eyes seemed sparkly and probably were. The world around me was vital again, and more than anything I felt my womanhood stirring and operating again. It was a private and precious time. I didn't want to lose it or diminish it by sharing it with anyone – least of all the man I was married to.

Walks in the woods were my escape. Long, meandering walks alone in the Adirondack Mountains. I'd say to myself *Go! Take off. Find a place you've never been before.* I'd walk for hours a day for what must have been a year. Early on, when the thrill of new love was too strong, I told my husband it was time for us to separate – this time for real. We'd talked about it for years, but the time had come. It only took 28 days of emails and new love for me to realize my marriage was over. 28 days! After 15 years of marriage. I see now that the quickness of it all, plus the lack of argument or resistance from either of us is a testament to how necessary the ending was. We were ready. Not sad. Not regretful or angry. Just fully aware of where we'd gotten to.

Should I have told him then? I wanted to. I needed to, and yet I didn't. I wanted to stay in my fragile, finite bubble of pleasure for as long as I could.

I've written about this so many times, thought about it endlessly, and the conclusion is always the same: I couldn't have and wouldn't have done anything differently. My lie, my withholding, was in service to my self. Joy had been absent for so long and the thrill of attraction was too strong for me to be able to do anything differently.

The soul searching I continue to do has become boring and tedious for me, for you, and for anyone I've leaned on to get me through the whiplash that's followed. Time seems to be the healer. Time has proven the reality of love, and that my lie was in service to that love.

Is there a better reason?

Where did you go when you had nowhere to go?

The Hour I First Believed

We're still here

The hour I first believed my mother was dying started with the hospice nurse finding a room for my sister Kari, and I to sit as she pitched the benefits of this hospice program. Hospice Nurse Robin put the royal-blue looseleaf binder on her lap, turning the pages as if she were a kindergarten teacher. I half expected her to pull out a pen and start writing letters upside down too.

In her pronounced southern accent, she said, "Oh hospice is not your grandmother's hospice anymore." She went on to say, "we care for the patient from the moment they enter the program—at home and at the hospice house. We know how important care is at this time of your mother's life. That people can live a long time, in the program, and often do." Nearly an hour has passed since I arrived and I'm having difficulty listening. I find myself drifting down to the pages of the binder and notice they have those adhesive-backed circles used to repair the holes of each page when the page has torn away from the binding clip. How is it I'm sitting here listening to this nurse talk of the advances in palliative care and this process of fixing the holes is still used— still necessary.

Though Robin tries to include me, I know she's really speaking to my sister who told her, deliberately, that she was a cardiac ICU nurse quickly establishing a medical bond between them. With no medical background I'm left to the musing of my brain as it tries to process the term "end stage." Even as they continue working through this new bond, I find thoughts in my mind and follow them in just the way we are told not to do when meditating. Had I known how, I think I would have started present-moment awareness immediately.

Consciously back in the room, once again seeing and hearing Robin as she flips the page and points to the pleasant, almost idyllic building surrounded by spring flowers and carefully-cared for shrubbery. She pulls the leave-behinds, the marketing material from the binder sleeve. I see her business card stapled neatly to the top. I take it from her hands as she and my sister continue to talk using phrases like, the meds didn't seem to 'touch' her, she is 94% occluded, and there shouldn't be any problem getting her approved for hospice at home.

How long did it take for me to believe Robin knew what was happening, understood what was best, was saying not just what I needed to hear, but that she was right about the care my mother would need for the time she had remaining? How long? It was nearly an hour the first part of which was filled with the barking cough of lungs that couldn't quite shake the pneumonia my mother developed. The last part an internal struggle where I found myself back in my mind following the only thought I had left. My mother is dying.

Who was the first person you loved who died? How old were you? Describe it as though you were that age? Then try it again from the point of view of where you are now.

Bear Hollow Road is long and steep heading up Mount Marcy. Trees drape over it from both sides, dense and full, colorful in the fall. Walking up is a workout; walking down is a relief. I park my car at the bottom, hide the keys on top of the front tire, then head up. When I lived with Ben, I could walk out our front door, turn right onto a path through the woods that led to a point a little higher than where I park my car now. I used to walk the dogs there a few times a day. When Theo was a baby, I'd say, "this is where God is for me" when we got to a certain curve in the path. There was something about the light that came through the pines, but also a knowing that something more than trees and light was happening there. I felt like I was being watched when I was at that spot. That onlookers were present, interested, but getting on with the life they were leading wherever it was they were. It was comforting. As though I had friends who were paying attention through that stretch.

My walks started getting longer and more rigorous when I met Michael. I needed to work harder. I walked higher and higher, deeper and deeper into the wilderness every day. I wanted to know for sure that if I went off the path I could still find my way home. I needed to know that I could get over my fear of being in an unknown place. More than anything I wanted to be somewhere where no one could find me; where I was truly alone. When I got to the highest, farthest away point on a given day, I'd sit, look up, rest, enjoy the absolute quiet that I found in the woods. I've always been happiest alone.

On a downhill walk months after I'd moved away from that house with Ben, I saw that light again coming through a different set of trees. This was brighter light than the rose-gold light streaming through the pines years before. It was pure sunlight, nothing particularly holy. I'd been filled with angst climbing up. I was tired of loneliness and confusion. Every moment of the previous six months I'd been thinking about what to do about loving Michael. Everything about it was wrong. Lots of people, whole families and an extended clan would be hurt if we came together. But not coming together was impossible. We were already together. We were already a pair despite 2000 miles between us. But when I saw that sun coming through the trees I made a choice. It was instantaneous. I chose to be joyful. I wanted love, and I wanted.

Have you ever been alone in the woods? What did it smell like?

Waking. So many sleeps. So many doubts. So many things to awake to, to believe in.

Yesterday, a long-time Christian woman, a woman who has worked at our church and who is now taking seminary classes and coordinating missions trips to Africa -- she looked at me and said, "This summer, in the midst of all this work, I had this thought that scared me: Is God even real?" She practically whispered the question. I know she expected me, as the pastor's wife, to look concerned and offer to pray, to assure her and to chastise her for even thinking such a thing.

Instead, I told her it was a pretty important question to ask. Then she was the one who looked surprised.

The faith tradition I was raised in emphasized a special moment of conversion -- a threshold of belief. And I think what they meant by conversion was something that happened to me about the age of four. But there was no way in the world that something that happened when I was four could be the whole shebang anymore than a first date or even a wedding day is the sum total of a marriage.

So there was the hour I first believed that I was truly, no-kidding, absolutely and at my core -- a sinner (to use the old theological word). I was 28. For while I had prayed the prayer at four and grew up singing the songs and memorizing the Bible, I did not truly believe there was anything wrong with my character. I was an obedient, compliant child. I always did what was asked of me. I was kind and generous. I was forgiving and patient. I was a good student and a good friend.

But at 20, I wondered if the protestant folks I'd grown up with had the best way of doing life. I put some distance between me and the church. I slowly drifted away from the circles of faith, and then I fell in love with a man who was married. It's a longer story than I have time to tell now, but a year after I met him, I was living with him and it had devastated my family. I had disappointed people who thought I would never be the one to step off of the straight and narrow. But their disapproval was not the thing that convinced me I had a deep flaw in my soul that I could not heal. It was not their pressure.

It was me. I was taking a class that summer on film noir -- and had spent the morning sitting in the dark watching Barbara Stanwick turn Fred McMurry from a Disney hero into a cold-blooded murderer. As I stepped out into the hot furnace of the parking lot, I felt like I was on the edge of an abyss. I never, ever thought that I would be the "other woman." Never, in a million years would I have done it. But here I was anyway. And if I could get here, what would keep me, in time, from killing someone?

And if I was capable of that, then grace had a whole new meaning. Than I really, really needed it. And I didn't deserve it. At all.

But there it was, before I even asked for it, I sensed it, I felt it. I was a hot mess. And I was loved anyway. By the maker of love Itself.

Describe God. Be specific.

If you don't believe in God, describe not believing.

(this may be a tough one, but see what happens if you try)

Knock on Wood

She was old enough to know better

The Next Right Thing

Before the next prompt, Charlotte read Mary Oliver's Poem "Don't worry" from Felicity *(2015) in which the poet says, "Don't worry, " followed by the question how long do you think it takes a saint to become a saint?*

How do you worry?

Annie chose "She Was Old Enough to Know Better" except all she heard was, "She Was Old."

My mother was old at 60. I am standing behind her, leading her into a private room at a Mexican restaurant, all of her family and friends gathered there to celebrate her 60th. I'm cautious, aware that this surprise may be too much for her. I'm protective, steering her through the crowd to the door of the room, easing her inside, delighting in her delight.

I miss her and yet I feel her everywhere still, even though it's been 12 years since she passed.

I talk to her on my morning walks. I ask her to help me with this and that. A chill runs through my body when I make these requests of her and of others who have gone on to the other side. I smile when it happens, when I feel the cold and know that I am surrounded by beings I cannot see.

My mom loved me. I know that. I wish she had done life differently—and yet. She died at 71, probably 40 years longer than she thought she would. Not a minute too soon or too late. Her body didn't serve her well. She didn't serve her well.

I learned from her example. Learned of self-destruction, of self-preservation, of making different decisions.

She loved me. I loved her. We're still connected even though I'll never again feel her touch—not in the palm of my hand, not on my shoulder. But still I know she's there.

What did you learn from your mom?

Write whatever comes to mind. If you mis-read or mis-hear a prompt, go with it. Some times the most interesting stuff comes from this kind of mistake.

I've been thinking a lot about the evolution of my sexuality, the randomness of the people who were involved. Some of them I didn't know well enough for them to touch me but I let them anyway. There was an adolescent necessity for those experiments.

Earlier, there was a natural evolution from touching Barbie's plastic breasts to playing doctor with Katie and Louise in the McConnell's attic. We touched each other in the dim light and enjoyed first-hand experience. I don't remember talking about it, planning it, or agreeing to it, we just did it. A few years later, Rob Camillino fumbled with my bra. I didn't know him. Hardly said a word to him before we were on someone's couch across from the school. I don't remember enjoying it or not enjoying it, I don't remember feeling guilty or not guilty. It was just something we did. A necessary step

I could go on with my list of boys and later, men. It's not an extra long list but it's long enough for me to wonder why? - not because of its length but because of its quality. There were no bad guys. No one hurt me with violence or aggression. But the list is full of men who were careless, men who had things on their mind that were more important than me. Looking back, I feel responsible for that. Despite every effort on my mother's part, I did not take her advice to respect my body. Each one of the men on my list (except for one, maybe two) was a lazy choice on my part. A choice to stick around rather than act on the fact that I wasn't getting what I needed.

Like Rob Camillino fighting the clasp on my bra, I just stayed at it as if I was obligated to be there, as though I had no choice. Getting to first base didn't require devotion it only required desire and my need to begin sexual exploration with the opposite sex.

I was old enough to know better later in my life, yet I didn't. If a man wanted me and was brave enough to ask, I said yes. And then I'd stick around because I didn't know what else to do; because I didn't know I needed more than a man wanting me in his life. I had to want him too.

If I'd been enjoying myself back then my list would look different to me now.

Where were you the first time you got to second base?
When did you do something you only half-wanted to do?

For decades, I've pulled over, removing dead animals from the roadways, whispering prayers for them, to them, settling their lifeless bodies into the grasses and expressing condolences to their friends and families who live in the trees, burrows, caves, but today on this chilly morning, a chestnut colored blur races in from the right side, and as I pump my brakes, swerve, there's a small thud, a very small thud.

With a look in the side mirror, I see a body flip up then down, my heart races, I turn around, go back, put my flashers on, walk to her. I see her right eye, otherwise she's perfect, no blood around her beautiful body, the body with the alternate black and white stripes down the sides of her back, the body with the rust colored tail, cheeks stuffed with nuts.

I pick her up, can hardly believe what' I've done, her body is warm, it's so warm, life was there just a moment ago.

I walk with her tiny body in my hand, and *it's so warm*, I balance on the stones that are slippery and shifting beneath my sneakers and take her to a maple tree, lay her down there, at the base, away from prying eyes, stroke her fur, so soft, so warm.

Nothing I say can take back what I've done, there's nothing to say, yet I do speak to her in the softest voice, I'm so sorry, I'm so sorry. I ask the angels of chipmunks to greet her, to escort her to the other side, to forgive me, to please, please forgive me.

Who have you taken care of? What happened to them?

Apparently, the softest voice is often mine. I was a shy kid. I watched a lot. I listened carefully, everywhere I went. I seldom spoke in the company of strangers.

I used to love sitting with the adults at the dining room table when my parents had friends over. The boys would go run around outside. My sister, who loved to chat, would head up to the dollhouse in our room with her friends. I would stay at the dining room table and listen.

They say children learn through play. That is probably true. But somehow, the world seemed too serious to me to play with toys all the time. Listening to the grown-ups, I could learn all kinds of important things. About the education system (my mom was a teacher and the district Superintendent was a family friend who she'd gone to high school with. His son was my brother's best friend.) About church politics (There were people grousing that the children had used hand motions when they sang a song on Sunday morning. Looked like dancing. It was actually sign language). About all kinds of things that I don't remember specifically but probably shaped what I expected from the world of adults.

I knew to keep quiet in these discussions, or they'd ask me to leave and I'd never hear the stories that held the secrets of survival in the real world.

I kept quiet at school, unless I knew positively that I knew the right answer to the question and then I raised my hand. I got really good at knowing the right answers.

I kept quiet on the playground with other kids. I didn't understand the games they played, the names they called each other, the way to fit in most of the time.

But walking home from school, straggling behind my brothers, I had long imaginary conversations. I was witty and astute. I knew what to say. I was even funny.

The only other time I could be loud was when I sang. I could be loud and confident because I knew the words and had just a good enough ear that I also knew the notes. And when I knew them well enough, it all started to feel spontaneous again.

For a long time as an adult, people have told me I have a soft voice. It always surprises me. I can hear myself. But I have not always wanted to be heard.

What do you want people to hear you say? Why don't you say it?

That Time in the Wilderness

I wake at four in the morning from another bad dream, my heart racing, eyes scanning the dark room. It takes a few moments to remember that I'm safe, to slow my breathing, my pulse.

I can feel the crisp air coming in through the screen and take a deep breath, cleansing my fears. The outdoors is right there, woods, I remind myself, available, safe, but still I lay there for a time unwilling to drift off again in case the dream resumes.

Then, from a short distance away, in the mountain, the contained wilderness, I hear a sound drifting down and through my open window, coyotes, yipping in some cacophonous celebration, greeting one another, teeth flashing, tails low and wagging, so full of wonderful life, that moment of pure silence before the dawn, before the world wakes, before cars and machinery and conversations take over and in that moment, listening to their ancient tongue, I feel safe again.

I'm not alone in the dark anymore.

What did you hear at 4 a.m.?

'Wilderness' is relative. Living in London, I came to think of Queen's Wood- an untamed, unmanaged park- as 'wilderness.' Given that Queen's Wood behind our flat was equidistant from three villages (Highgate, Muswell Hill and Crouch End) each within walking distance from one another, I could never get lost. If I had strayed off the path, the sound of bumper to bumper traffic on the Archway, also known since the Roman occupation as the Great North Road, would direct me.

Getting lost was not an option, and yet, the Hansel and Gretel nature of the woods (the wolf... where was the wolf?) was unsettling. The ungroomed nature of the woods juxtaposed with the density of the city was as startling as a hand on the top of a hot woodstove.

The deciduous trees were tall and dense. During the plague years, thousands of bodies were supposedly dumped in this patch. Perhaps the robust trees had fed on the decayed bodies. Leaving a leaf-strewn path, you were on your own.

If you left the Highgate Tube and walked towards Muswell Hill, you would see a gingerbread café on the right. Walking towards the café, you would pick up the path just past the café. If you were to keep walking some distance along the path, you would see a clearing surrounded by 13 ancient oak trees off to the right. Local lore had it, that on a full-moon night, local Druids would gather to invoke the past.

Living just south of Queen's Wood, I would cut through the woods to reach the Tube station. Doing so I would pass an old man who had built a cardboard shelter and was 'sleeping rough."

Again... the juxtaposition of the civilized and wild. Wild and lost.

I used to know the London Tube map by heart. What did you know by heart?

I climbed and climbed and climbed in those days. Day after day. The end of my marriage, the beginning of a new life I didn't understand or know how to make real. So I climbed and climbed some more. Everyday I went further, higher, further, just to know that I could. Wanting to scare myself and then overcome the fear. I'd climb until the fear of being lost outweighed the longing to overcome my fear. That day in the wilderness, I found an ancient, empty creek that was nearly dry but damp from recent rain. The sun was shining in rays through pine trees. When I got to a place that was as far away as I was willing to go, I took my clothes off. All of them. Adding more fear to my already pumping heart. Wondering if someone would see me. The odds were long. Naked. I lay down on a smooth, damp rock by the empty old stream. I felt the heat and my skin. The sun. The prickers from a nearby bush. I felt alive and I felt brave.

What did you do that surprised and pleased you?

Doing Without

What can I do without?

Well-meaning friends would say that I should have washing machine and dryer on the premises. Typically, I do our laundry in our primary residence, our family home in Penrose. We still get our mail there, and picking up the mail necessitates a weekly visit. While I am there, I do laundry. Yes, it would be more convenient to launder clothes in our retirement home, but it has never been an issue.

Nearly every relative and friend sighs and moans about the laundry problem. They go so far to berate Mark for abusing me – denying me… every woman's right to have a washer and dryer close at-hand. Friends shake their heads. They feel sorry for me. Their hearts break for me. What they do not realize is I do not have a washer/dryer issue.

To hear them talk, you would think that I had an old-fashioned washboard in the back yard where my reddened hands and swollen knuckles would scrub the grubby Levis of my husband and the hired man. Listening to my friends' version of events, you would thing that after milking the cows and gathering eggs at dawn, I had to make soap before doing the wash. And then, laundry washed but lacking a real clothes line, I would have to walk about the yard laying the wet clothes over fences and shrubs where all the neighbors could comment on my unimaginative underwear.

Contrary to the opinion of friends who like to make their issues… my issues, I can do without a washing machine at present. I have other things I cannot do without.

I cannot do without coffee. I like it black and strong. Full-flavored with an aroma that hints of South America and Juan Valdez.

Most of all, I would miss my friends who fill me up with love and compassion and forgiveness. These same friends challenge me to be better than I am … introduce me to new ideas… and believe in me more than I believe in myself.

When did you follow the wrong advice?

Last night, PBS broadcast the second of two programs on pre-natal surgery, something I think I'd heard of before but hadn't given much thought to. Babies in the womb who have a condition that's fixable can be operated on to increase their chances of living a normal or better life. One of the children they followed on the show was a little girl named Lily. Her mother was un-married and the father had abandoned her when he heard the baby had a massive tumor growing in her throat that was overflowing from her mouth. The young mother went to Philadelphia Children's Hospital to see if the doctors there could help her.

I watched as the surgical team removed a mass from Lily's face that was nearly as big as her 6-inch fetal body. Last night we saw her at 4-months with a Joker style smile that was about to be repaired in the second radical surgery of her life. There were other surgeries on the show. Other fetuses, moms and dads in doctor's offices, surgical suites, other anaesthetized children, MRIs, scans, all things I lived through fourteen years ago. I saw things last night I hadn't seen myself but have often imagined, like the clear tape with the width and heft of packing tape that's put over the baby's eyes during surgery to protect them from whatever might spill or splatter while in the OR; or the tattoos that are meticulously placed on the baby's skin to show the surgeon where to cut and how to fold that skin so that everything looks good when the baby has healed; or the tug and the pull of stitches that go deep into the baby's body when they're sewing him back up.

I've imagined these things many times. I made myself imagine them when Theo was going through even more demanding surgeries. His belly was opened wide, his guts removed so that the grapefruit size tumor attached to his liver, his heart, and his gall bladder could be cut away and removed. The day of that surgery, I lived inside my over-sized parka sitting in the waiting room, imagining every step of Theo's day. From the moment he left my arms, already sedated and gone from me, to the moment I saw him again 9 hours later – bloated, bruised, lying on a gurney with nine lines of critical connection to keep him alive, and a doctor hand-pumping air into his body until a ventilator could be re-attached in the ICU across the street. An ambulance was waiting as he flew by me helpless in the lobby of Sloan Kettering. He was alive. It was all I had and it was a lot.

I knew exactly what those parents on TV were feeling. Terror. Shock. Confusion. Disbelief. Love so deep and non-negotiable that all the tests Theo, Ben and I were going through didn't feel like tests, they felt like life. It's what we did.

Sitting in front of the TV, tears streaming down my face, mine had been a time of love more than anything else. I live without that kind of love now.

When did you live without love?

*

My thirteenth year started with a short sale of the house my family had built in a small town in North Dakota. It was supposed to be our home place for the rest of our lives. But a second mortgage had been taken out to keep my dad's business running. And then the business went bankrupt.

We moved to a working class suburb of Chicago, a place called Addison. A family friend was a pastor of a church on Army Trail Road. He was not using the parsonage next door, so the church let us rent it for a song. Within months of moving in there, my parents divorced after 20 years of marriage.

My dad installed garage doors to support himself and pay child support. My mother could only get work as a substitute teacher. Somehow my mother found another side job, cleaning a Xerox office building after hours five nights a week. My sister and I helped her out, emptying trash cans and cleaning toilets.

Every penny counted. That was the year I learned to look at price tags and curb my own appetites. We had never been wealthy before, but it simply facilitated typical limits on childhood selfishness: I could choose two toys, not five. I could have one treat a weekend, not endless indulgence.

But that thirteenth year, it was entirely different. Peanut butter and cheap bread (past its "sell by" date, so half price), macaroni and tomato paste. My skin was developing its adolescent oiliness, breaking out. But even the cheapest antiseptic cleanser and a bag of cotton balls was outside the budget.

My mother, exhausted as she was, tried to make it fun, tried to turn shopping at garage sales and second hand stores into a treasure hunt. To this day, though, I do hate going to department stores and malls. They seem filled with overpriced excess, and mannequin after mannequin silently declaring that they, who have no voice and no soul, have enough -- and never have to do without.

What did you eat as a kid? Fried Bologna? Moon Pies?

The Corner Store

Habits of Transition

The corner store was a block from my house and at the top of my friend Nancy's street. It was our first corner store, the closest one to our house and situated almost halfway between my two best friends' houses in a safe neighborhood, a small town where everyone knew everyone.

It was the place to go for Wonder Bread and milk and candy. It was a converted gas station – painted white cinder block building, darkened room for the store with only one case/counter – and the room where the car bay had been was closed off. The smell of gasoline and oil lingered. The gas pumps outside were red and I don't think they were operational any more.

A bigger store, the Corner Dairy, was another block away. Family owned and operated, at first it was a wooden building with a couple of aisles. It was our stopping point on the way home from school every day. We'd buy Fresca or Pepsi and Cheetos, Fritos, maybe some candy. They had baseball trading cards and Beatles cards and a rack of magazines like Tiger Beat and Seventeen. Playboy and cigarettes and cigars were kept behind the counter. Mr. C and his wife watched over us kids – not that anyone I knew was a shoplifter but you could feel them, vigilant, when we lingered over the penny candy for too long.

The prices there, my mom and dad said, were too high so we didn't buy much there except our after school snacks, maybe bread and milk. Over the years, the family that owned the store gradually grew it until now it's a full-fledged market with a few long aisles stocked with all the groceries you could need.

My family moved away from that street over 15 years ago so I haven't been back there. I'd be surprised if it's even run by the same family now.

Another fragment – there was another market too – the meat market – wooden floor boards creaked, darkened room, cases filled with roasts, chicken, fresh cuts, strange pickled things in cloudy jars.

Which did you like better, Oreos or Hydrox?

Wonder Bread or Pepperidge Farm?

Hellman's or Miracle Whip?

In Jamestown, North Dakota, when I was about nine or ten, both my parents sang in the church choir. In the spring that year, the choir director decided to do a big choral "cantata" — a production of sacred music interspersed with dramatic readings of scripture passages and personal testimonies.

It was a big deal for our little church. And the director took his music very seriously. So in addition to the regular Wednesday night choir rehearsals, there was a month of long Sunday afternoon practices. With both my parents in the choir, we kids and the kids of several other families, came and had the run of the church basement.

We really could do anything we wanted, as long as we didn't break anything or interrupt practice. There were massive games of hide-n-seek. Then a complicated, stealthy version of indoor capture-the-flag. We explored all the cupboards in the church kitchen, the janitor's closet, the back row of the balcony, and one week we even discovered that the secret door into the baptismal was unlocked. This was a discovery! And we took turns quietly crawling into the deep bathtub that opened up to the sanctuary from behind a screened window above the organ.

Eventually, we got bored exploring the nooks and crannies of the building. Besides, the weather was warm and fine. The air smelled like damp dirt and things were starting to turn green, so we went out and explored the neighborhood.

Down the street, around the block from the church, on the south end of Main Street where we'd rarely drive, there was a gas station with the little requisite store attached.

I don't remember who said it. Maybe Landon Nitzchke, who was always more courageous than most of us. Or Brenda Benson, whose mom, Shirley, played the piano for the choir. But someone said, "Let's buy something."

Standing out on the sidewalk, we all dug into our pockets, scoured the curb for dropped pennies, and pooled all the loose change we could find: 65 cents. Then, we walked into the store and searched the candy aisle for what we could afford.

It was the first time I had ever been in a store, let alone a candy store, without parental supervision, limits or finances. We were making our own decision. And no one could tell us what to do!

Finally, we settled on two boxes of candy I'd never had before. Mike and Ike's were pill-shaped, multicolored fruit flavored chews. The other box was a cinnamon flavored version of the same candy, all bright red.

We walked the few blocks back to church, sharing the boxes back and forth as we went, plotting how to collect more loose change by next Sunday. Savoring the sweet, sticky taste of freedom.

What's in your wallet?

*

I was seven when we moved to Breesport, a small Upstate New York town boasting only of two churches, a school, a post office, the Chemung County Poor House, and Elliott's – a small, two-aisle-wide grocery store.

Although the town was rural and a bit backwoods (every child had lice at least once a school year), I was excited. Finally, after living in the two-bedroom apartment above my grandparent's house and depending on Grandpa or Mon's older brother for transportation, we had our very own large house and our very own maroon-colored Chevy.

Mom was not one to put her foot down, but before we moved in, she insisted on indoor plumbing. I was too young to understand the dynamic, but Daddy was probably regretting that he had been so rash to marry an uppity, college-educated woman with high-falutin' ideas.

And so we had indoor plumbing. It was only a couple of blocks to Main Street and Elliott's store which had just about everything: white bread, milk, flour, canned vegetables and toilet paper. Desires were fewer in 1950.

How honored I felt to be asked to pick up the mail on my way home from school. The heritage, brass boxes were faced with a peephole window a combination dial. Twirling the knob right and then left and then right again, I felt quite full of myself as I pulled out the mail.

Sometimes, Mom asked me to pick up something at the small, two-aisle-wide store. Picking up the requested item, I'd walk to the cash register where I'd lift my chin and say, "Charge it to our account." Doing so, I felt responsible and all-powerful. First, the cashier knew who I was, and second, she knew we would pay our bill at the end of the month.

We were on our way… into the middle class!

Did you ever have lice or some other gross thing that gives you the creeps now?

Did it give you the creeps then?

It's Packed Away in A Box

listening…

61

When Debra heard this prompt she said, "I just finished a piece called "It's Packed Away in a Box"! Can you use it?" I said, "Sure." What's different reading a finished piece VS a quickly written prompt response?

"It's Packed Away in a Box"

I called my mom on Friday night. I don't call at a regular time but I try to speak with her every week. My sister and her family had just left town for the weekend – Diane usually checks in on them because she lives nearby – so I teased mom, "Are you lonely yet?"

She has an easy laugh, my mom does, though she's got less to feel amused about these days. My dad has Alzheimer's or dementia, we're not sure which because he refused to complete the diagnostic tests a couple of years ago.

Doesn't really matter, I suppose. She calls it "All-timers" and hushes her voice on our phone calls when she wants to share some details of his latest comments or confusions. "He's so forgetful. I try to be patient but it's hard when he asks me the same things over and over and over …"

A lot of times when we talk now it's about their doctor's appointments, ailments, medications. Maybe news of an occasional outing or visit. But, on Friday night, we somehow bypassed the usual reporting and had a lot of fun, laughing and remembering happier times.

I mentioned to mom that my hair has grown really long again. "It's probably as long, or longer, than when I was in high school," I said.

"I still have your hair, you know. Remember when you got it cut?"

Surprised, I said, "Really? Wow. Where is it?"

She had given me a lot of my childhood and teenage things when they moved 15 or so years ago – *The Better Homes and Gardens* Baby Book she had filled in with my vital statistics, ink print of my foot from the hospital records and progress (first smile, first word, lost her first tooth), my Girl Scout book, some of my baby clothes and my bronzed baby shoe – but not my hair from when I'd suddenly cut it short.

"In the lock box."

I laughed. "The *lock* box?!"

All I could think about was, 'there's so much stuff in their house already. There's more in there, too?'

It was daunting, all the silk flower arrangements and clothes, not to mention antiques, jewelry, knick knacks, furniture, boxes of photographs … it would take years to figure out what to do with it all when the time came.

"Oh god, what *else* is in there?"

"Oh, I don't know. The deed to the house, our birth certificates, important papers." She paused, "Maybe your hair isn't in there, I don't know. It's here, some place, though."

It was disconcerting, thinking about a long shank of now-faded hair, sitting in a box somewhere, who knows where? Then I remembered that I had saved some hair too.

"Now that we're talking about this, mom, I have one of Diane's curls saved too." It's in a dark green jewelry box – I can see it clearly, a lid that snaps shut, with green velvet lining. It was the box from the gold locket Aunt Charlotte and Uncle Roy gave to me for high school graduation. "It's in a jewelry box, but I'm not sure where it is, exactly. It's here some place ..." echoing her. We were both laughing.

My mom liked it, that I had one of sister's curls. When Diane was a toddler, she had a mass of golden brown curls all over her head. And every day, when my mom or I dressed her in one of her cute little outfits, there were yarn bows or ribbons or clips to match what she was wearing.

I was 12 when Diane was born and spent a lot of time playing with her and taking care of her throughout my teenage years, until I went away to college.

And, despite knowing there were so many things saved in every corner and drawer and shelf of our home, I liked knowing my hair was there too. Some day I'd find it, probably when mom and dad were gone, and I'd remember this laughing conversation and how mom and I both knew that we saved too much stuff.

Imagine being on the phone with your mom. What did she say? How did you respond? Use dialogue.

I love that dress. Still have it. I wore it to a fund raising concert that was given for me after Theo died. It was my maternal grandmother's: black taffeta with painted red and purple flowers all over it. The pedals are outlined in gold. Little black velvet dots meander around the skirt. Underneath, the petticoats pile up, itch, and make a swooshing sound on the floor without the right heels. Mine were just a little too low so I heard myself wherever I went.

I would love to have seen Gammy, my grandmother, wearing this dress. She was flamboyant and beautiful. In one picture of her with my grandfather, she's wearing a floppy blue hat with an 8" rim. In the ribbon around her hat, she's planted a big fabric flower that drapes down around her forehead. She's smiling from ear to ear as my grandfather leans into her.

When I was little, my father called me Little Gammy. I'm not sure why. I've never been flamboyant. I should ask him what he saw back then. Maybe it was her girlish ways. I certainly had that trait even as I was climbing trees and playing kick the can for hours in the middle of Hill Road.

Gammy made this sound with her mouth. She'd pucker her lips, force air through them making a high-pitched "bweeeeeep" whenever she wanted us to laugh. She'd giggle with her whole body then start to laugh, her shoulders shaking all the while. Grandpa was more serious, a Colonel in the Army, fought both wars. He adored her wild spirit and encouraged her to let it out. They had regular parties, scotch and pretzels every afternoon. Restaurants and friends were a big part of their life. His father had died when he was eight He was an only child so he was the man in the family very early on. Gammy gave him the childhood he'd missed, I guess. Their first child died when he was two. He was born with Spina Bifida, a spinal imperfection a person can survive these days. My mother was born when he was one. She has no memory of him, of course, but he was always there. Maybe I'm imagining that.

When was a dress more than a dress?

Abigail Thomas sent a new poem the day our group was meeting so I used it as a prompt.
*Her original title was "**A Why Bother to Write it Poem**" so that was the prompt.*
Now it's called:

"Lament"

It's a man and a woman and they've climbed to the top of a mountain and it's evening and from where they stand they can see whole worlds and some tiny bright cities and since he had coaxed her up this high, because he wanted to show her everything, he had his arms around her tightly because she was afraid of falling. And the sun actually did go down on their right at the exact moment the moon rose on their left, and this would have happened anyway, they both knew that, still they were glad to have seen it together. Whether they lay down and made love or did not make love under a billion stars is if no real interest to anyone (there being no small boys present) and who they were, and whether he knew the names for everything and if she loved lavender, if it rained, all these details vanish like everything else, it happens all the time, you know, the sun goes up and comes down it rains, we button and unbutton our clothes and turn on our sides to make love because all warm animals need other warm animals right from the beginning or they go crazy and die so if he had green eyes and she had blue and if they loved or did not love each other for good reasons or bad and if they used the old words and did or did not make promises nobody keeps, no matter, we'll let it go, no matter.

Sometimes we read something to one another and no prompt is offered. A quiet settles over us and no prompt is necessary.

If you're uncomfortable with silence, describe it...

Zoe and I run out into the early March wind at seven in the morning, we trot down the road, she stopping to pee, looking up and around, running again with her left rear leg still up and peeing, 'come on' she implores, we head to the corner of Swift Hollow, she pulling me, her little body, propelled forward, ears blowing just a bit, making the soft waves of those ears, ripple with the breeze.

I hear the crows at my house, raucously calling to me, reminding me that I hadn't fed them yet, hadn't laid out the unsalted nuts in the shell, the kernels of hard deer corn, leftover cat and dog food, seeds, fruit, whatever looks good and viable.

I glance back toward my house as the road disappears and Zoe propels us forward, 'come on'. I'm not used to leaving the house before feeding the wild but this little one is my charge for the week and so I follow her as she weaves her way through damp leaves, placing her nose in those leaves for any hint of another animal, always moving forward.

I hear a crow overhead, look up, and there's one of my crows who flies directly over us, cawing, perhaps wondering why I'm heading away from the mountain, away from their feeding spot they share with other birds, squirrels, deer, turkeys, chipmunks, and maybe that crow is sending the signal to her friends, 'she's here, I'll try to lead her back'.

On the next foray into the weeds and halfhearted trail that quickly leads to deadfall too dense and vast to scale, Zoe and I turn back, making a game of it, let's head home, I excitedly say to her.

As we wind our way back up, mountain now growing closer again, the crows begin cawing, swooping down lightly, rapid clicks of their bill, and as we turn into the driveway, they fly low past us, leading me to their clearing between the trees.

I open the door and Zoe zips inside the house while I head back outside with pots and bags filled with food, talking with the crows, they responding from the trees, the squirrels now swinging from branches and racing head first down the tree trunks to the ground and I realize, not for the first or second or thousandth time, that no matter where I am in this world, the animals will always fly me home.

Have you ever talked to animals?

I have been reading Mary Oliver and almost every page gives a deep look into the beautiful soul of something nobody ever cares to look at. The things that happen anyway. But still, she is delighted to witness it and then sing a song for us, made up from her ball-of-twine words.

It arrests me. So much happens in any present moment, it's startling.

Last week we sat at breakfast before Andrea left for Austin, and she and her dad named off all the people they know who've died of horrible cancers or sudden accidents in the last year. Then there was the strange sniper shots that have broken car windows and killed a bicyclist along I-25 this summer. The terrorist attacks on tourists, sunning on Middle Eastern beaches. All the things that can break and tear, destroy and kill. And who knows when or where it happens next?

Andrea, the night before, had mentioned how she didn't have insurance in this month between ending one job and starting the next. "Maybe, I should get online now, get some kind of short term coverage. I mean, before I go off and drive 900 miles…" And all the things that can go wrong crowded around the kitchen table in the silent moment when none of us made eye contact.

That's when her dad said that the only way to not go crazy was to stay in the present moment. I nodded, felt my shoulders relax, my heart slow a little. Until I realized that even this — this split second. This paper thin slice of all time is so densely populated with miracles and spectacles.

The citronella ants in the foundation, the doves on the power lines, the seeds already softening in the ground since I planted them this morning, the words taking shape beneath pens, the hundreds of skin cells dying off. The hundreds just coming to be. Oxygen taken into a dog's lungs while she dreams of catching a rabbit on the run.

A hundred million high wire acts happening just now. A hundred million more in the next moment. Why bother to write a poem? Why bother at all since none of it matters?

I cannot help myself. Because the more I see or taste, hear or believe, the more beautiful and real and sweet the nonsense is. I care less and less these days about leaving a mark. More and more, I am willing to be the page on which the lines are written.

Start a paragraph with "I have been thinking." Start another one with "I've been thinking."

Why bother to write it? You can't, won't read it. Why bother to tell you I meant no harm? Why bother to care that you care?

Why bother to write a poem that would try to explain the unexplainable?

I want you to know I'm happy, really happy, because I know that at some point you would have cared. You would have wanted that for me. But I can't call you up. I could, sure, but I can't. I would open a door I slammed shut. It would say to you that I want something I don't: You.

Why bother to rhyme words? To speak from the heart? To tell you I wasn't lying when I said I'd love you forever? Forever, as it turned out, was much shorter than I could have imagined. I didn't lie. I didn't pretend to love you. I didn't fake my way through our marriage. I delighted in you. I loved you. I was grateful for you.

But you wanted to keep me and I couldn't be kept.

"I'm not ready to say 'thank you,'" you once said, and then went on to tell me that my leaving invited others—wonderful others—into your existence.

I knew this would happen, but of course it wasn't for me to say. It wasn't for me to ask, "Aren't you better off?" even if I already knew the answer.

I do wish you happiness. I wish you great happiness and contentment. I still cheer you on. I cast well wishes into the Universe, hoping they'll land in your lap.

But I won't beg you to forgive me. It's unnecessary. It's counterproductive. But if I could, I would say to you that you were wonderful. You were perfect.

For that space in time, we were.

Who hurt you when they didn't listen?

It has no weight. No substance. No matter. No real beginning or end. It just is. This love. This madness of attraction. It's unlike the rejection of the past when my body wasn't good enough for him. Wasn't the body he wanted to touch, to breathe in, to consume.

I want to understand it all. Why it was so awkward and so good to see Ben again. And yet I was afraid of him. He noticed it, mentioned it even. Said, "you look like you're seeing a monster," and I said, "yes, I am." And we both laughed. Me having just blown a big green bubble of Trident gum as he turned into the gas station and pulled up to the far side of the pump I was using. Me standing there blowing a bubble, him pulling up in a new truck. "Just got it," he says. And all I can think is *lucky you* because he has some money I still think belongs to me and I haven't let go of that fact yet. So I remove the gum and laugh. "This is so tacky, me standing here blowing bubbles when I haven't seen you for four years. It's a crummy habit I've developed." He says, "plenty of people chew gum, ya know, it's ok," but it's not ok with me. I don't want to be chewing gum when I'm talking to the man I married twenty-one years ago; the man I haven't seen for four years, five and a half since we lived together somewhat happy, somewhat empty, wandering and lost because neither of us had the partner we needed. Neither of us had been touched with any tenderness for over ten years, neither of us able to see a future together, both of us honest about the hopelessness of it all.

So I didn't want to be chewing gum. I took it out and looked for a trashcan. There weren't any. They must have been removed because people were leaving their household garbage there. Instead I rolled the green ball between my fingers while we reacquainted ourselves, me and this man I loved all along.

The visit was good. I got to say the things I've needed to say these last four years. Not with vengeance or anger but with gentleness. "Ya know, Ben, it was really hard to be #2 all those years." I told him that because I knew he'd never understood. His eyes filled with tears. He crinkled up his mouth that way he does and nodded as if to say *I know. You always* were #2. And then I said, "I loved you, ya know." And he crinkled up his mouth again. And I could feel myself wishing he'd say "I loved you too" but I knew he wouldn't and I was right. He said, "but we had Theo together and that was really good," and I agreed because it *was* good. We both smiled. We were his parents me and Ben. And if Theo were here, we would still be a family because neither of us could have broken his heart for anything or anyone.

We hugged. I didn't know if I would ever do that again, if I would want to, or if I would take a step away from him. But we did, twice. He initiated both times and both times he held me tight while I rolled the gum in my free hand.

When did you see someone you thought you'd never see again?

Did you move towards them, or away?

Unpacking from the Trip

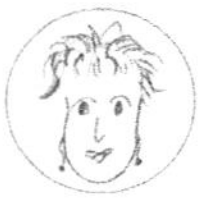

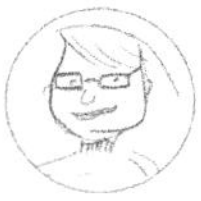

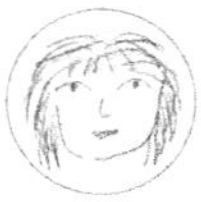

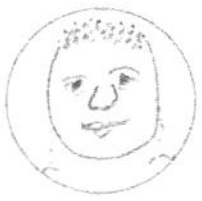

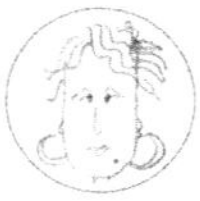

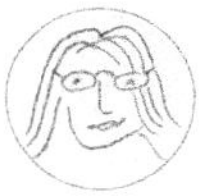

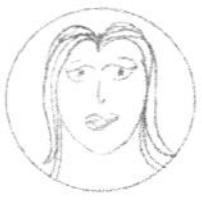

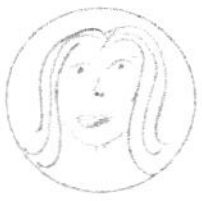

While I can't remember all the circumstances surrounding the hotel stay last summer, I can remember the exaltation. There was the huge bed, two huge beds, dozens of pillows, a soft brown comforter and blankets of varying shades of oranges and yellows, an enormous television, room service, insulated quiet, privacy.

I opened my suitcase and took out the bare essentials, knowing that I'd only have a few hours to enjoy this array of..what ..this dreamy way of living.

The king bed near the window was for the suitcase, the clothes, the other king bed was for me to luxuriate in so I flopped on top of those colorful blankets, spread my arms wide, smiling at the ceiling.

I kept reading the menus of the different cafes and restaurants, imagining what it'd be like to live here for a week, what would I order on Tuesday, Wednesday? Would I have them deliver some scrumptious dessert at ten pm?

There was certainly nothing very interesting outside, a nearby airport, the Colorado heat, and a busy road within feet. No, this was about living inside luxury.

People were walking quietly down the hall in expensive clothing, no doubt living extravagant lives, residing in wealthy communities with manicured lawns, driving Priuses, ringing bells for tea.

Of course, none of that was probably true; most of these people were tourists, on hard earned vacations, indulging in fantasies, like me.

But those several hours, waiting for an early morning flight are etched in me, the scent of the room, the feeling of another way of living, a way of living that I'd never really want, for I'm not easily transfixed by the indoors or luxury, but when my friend, Mary and I meet in the hall at three in the morning to head to the airport and catch the flight back to New York, I tuck a memory into my pocket, a pen which I still have in my desk drawer, it reads 'the Radisson'.

Did you ever stay somewhere that was fancier than you're used to? Why were you there?

Dirty... clean... sort of clean. Hum.m.m.m... clean enough? I bring the shirt to my nose and smell it.

I'm unpacking from a week-long trip to the Gulf Coast. I pack small; regardless, my red carry-on (handwoven by natives in Peru) seems to expand beyond the dimensions of the cloth. The zipper may expand too. I see a small bag, but opening it is like opening a magician's bag of tricks. I open the bag and out fly a dozen doves.

How could so many things come out of something so small? And why did I take so much clothing in the first place? Why did I think I needed the silk blouse? Perhaps the silk blouse fell under the category of 'always be prepared.' I had the silk blouse but I also... please remember that I was going to the Gulf Coast... I also took my LL Bean coat purported to be good to minus 40 degrees.

And I took hiking boots. And black palazzo pants. And a light-weight, hip length blouse to hide my stomach. The blouse features large flowers on a white background. I am not a flower girl. I probably bought the blouse at Goodwill. Perhaps it had a good label. And the price was probably good. I can easily be swept away by a good bargain.

I packed the blouse because it was summer-weight and would cover my stomach. But get this.

When I am home, I don't tuck the blouse in because my stomach *could* be flatter. But my sister's stomach is seriously more Rubenesque than mine/. And so...

At my sister's house (that would be my sister with the larger stomach) I tucked the blouse in.

I tucked the blouse in and as I was doing so, my motivation for doing so slapped me in the face. Sibling rivalry had raised its ugly head.

It was a na.. na...nah...na... na... hah moment. I recognized my motivation. I winced. And still I tucked my blouse in.

It was sort of payback time for all the times my sister beat me at cards. The times her grades were better than mine. The times my mother asked me why I couldn't apply myself to my studies like my sister Christine.

What's the least you need?

What did you wear to cover yourself?

I waited to unpack my bag, hoping that I could somehow slip back to the airport, back into the writing life I left behind in Westcliffe, Colorado. I was here but I wanted to be there. Ken knew he had lost me and so the fight began to keep me. In his asking, "Are we altered?" he already knew the answer.

He picked me up at the airport and we arrived home after 10, both of us fearful, worried about what had happened in my honesty. In sending Ken that essay I had unleashed all that I had kept hidden, even from myself. It wasn't about my sexuality. It was about the truth of me.

I couldn't have known then that I would go back to Westcliffe, alone, months later, but there was part of me that didn't want to unpack the bag. If I unpacked it would mean that part of my life I had unearthed in Westcliffe would be hidden again. By unpacking I would say, "I'm staying" when I didn't want to.

I wanted to be back in Westcliffe, back in the beauty of that place, back in the bubble of creativity that the workshop organizers, teachers and participants had created. I wanted to be with them, all of them—the writers, and of course Michelle.

Oh my God what was that? What happened there? Why there? Why with her? Why with a "her?" What were we to do with the electricity that shot out of us, connecting in some place neither of us could see but we most definitely felt?

God I loved it. I hadn't felt that alive in a long time. Not just across from her at Sangrita's, but in the cocoon of Westcliffe.

Have you ever been somewhere that changed your life? Have you ever been somewhere that felt so good that you wanted to stay? What did it feel like to feel so good?

As Penny gave the prompt this morning I looked for my calendar so I could see into my future but the calendar isn't here. Did I leave it in the suitcase that I stashed on the top shelf in the laundry. I'll need it, so hopefully it's not at my parents' house on the bureau in what we call Dede's Room. My gloves are missing too. Not the gloves that mom gave me seven or eight years ago, which I have proudly not lost yet (or have I?) but the ones I got from Ben's mom when she died eleven years ago.

This most recent trip was the first trip in a long time that TSA hasn't opened my suitcase at some point and checked out its contents. I'm not sure why they look at mine but my guess is that it's the weight (many books inside) or the metal objects they see when they scan it. (Thumb drives, tape recorders, microphones, whatever). They always leave a nice note saying they've been there, and I always wonder if some guy in the sub-basement of whatever airport I've travelled through has checked out my underwear while he's in there. What would he say? *This girl needs an upgrade* or *how does she expect to get laid wearing this shit?*

When I first met Michael, well, even before I met him, I did a full undergarment overhaul. I even went to Victoria's Secret and felt sexy doing so. No matter they had no bras for women like me, no underwear a woman could wear without feeling like the wedgies given by a younger brother many years ago. I did buy a bathrobe, though, and still feel very elegant and feminine wearing it….when I do, which is rarely. I found the underwear I could comfortably wear at Macy's: Jockey's in a nice polyester/fake silk fabric, and bras sized 36A that were still not a little too big for me. What I discovered is that those over-sized bras could be worn anyway and make me look like I have more than I do. I didn't want to trick anybody, least of all Michael, but they weren't *that* oversized, and they did make me look more like the woman I thought he was hoping to see. Anyway, the point is, I need yet another overhaul. I'm still wearing those same underpants and banged up bras. They're stretched and stained and generally misshapen but they're what I've got. I take my cue from Michael. His underpants are even older. If he wants me in newer gear, he's gonna have to have some too.

Wait….that's not true and this is memoir: his underwear IS new. I've bought him rather expensive Under Armour underwear every year for Christmas. He loves wearing them and he looks pretty good in them too. Shoot. I've gotta go shopping! It's time. But this time, no bras. I'm getting back to my no-bra days. Undershirts that sort of support are much more comfortable and I no longer care about filling up my shirts a little better, at least not all the time.

The unpacking thing is mostly in my head. When I get back I debate everything: why am I here? What am I doing with my life? How can I make enough money to buy that house I found a mile down the street from my parents? Is it the right house? Could I pull it off? Would Michael be willing? What am I doing here? What am I doing with my life? etc etc. It takes about a day to run through the questions in the unending way that I do the day I get back. By this morning, I was thinking how nice it is to wake up with deep silence around me, dark skies, two dogs snoring nearby, and a big, hunky fella lying next to me. Michael told me yesterday that everyone he knows is stuck where they are regardless of their finances. For one reason or another they can't just get up and go to some supposedly better place. He's right.

When you were a kid, what did you notice when you got home from being away? What did your house smell like? Where did the light come in? Which lamp was left on? Describe it all, every detail you can think of.

If this were a spelling Bee what word would knock you out of the competition?

After the spelling bee prompt, Penny read a snippet from Christian Wiman's book, My Bright Abyss, *in which he suggests that we not only accept but also "come to praise" the fact that we're never going to find a right way that will work for us every time.*

What is it that you must realize?

'Conscience.' That's the word I have to think about it. I remember 'Con-Science' which is how I remember how to spell it. I like how it sounds too: Con-Science. Like there's an art to being a con, which there is. But it's the related words that would knock me out of a spelling bee:

'consciousness' for instance.

That words a killer. I don't even think I've spelled it right here. It never looks right to me. When I write it with a pen the odds of my success are better. Spelling it out loud under pressure would terrify me and guarantee my failure.

Bruce Hornsby wrote a great song about a guy named Tom and his rival who wins the Spelling Bee. The killer word for Tom's nemesus was banana. He spelled it:

B-a-n-a-n-a-n-a

not because he didn't know how to spell it but because he was so nervous he added the extra n-a.

I wonder if you even noticed it was spelled wrong? It's hard to see with a word like 'banana.'

A related word, 'consciousness,' is a word I'm working on on two levels. Trying to spell it is the least of my worries. Learning to be it is another thing all together. I went to bed last night thinking about it as a matter of fact. Not how to spell it but how to have more of it in my life. My mind was busy, busy, busy, like that other kind of bee. I was aware of my busy-ness, so that's good I guess, but what I also saw was that I'm short-tempered and just plain short when my mind is busy. I hurry. I take on too much. I dream about the big, successful finish I'll have when one of a dozen ideas in my head finally takes off. I stop myself: *don't think like that. Don't think big. It always take you off course, you invest too much. You give away too much, you distract yourself from the quiet work you really need and want to do*. All of this I saw like a mirror that goes on forever. My mind has always worked this way. I'm conscious of that. I'm aware. And I like it this way. Some times. Not all the time, but some times.

What's your wildest dream? How would life change if it came true?

I have a similar problem except it's the word 'conscientious' that screws me up

How reassuring to know that there is no right way. I don't know who said this, but if I were to get a tattoo, I'd have the saying inked in black on my left shoulder and I'd always wear sleeveless blouses. I'd be swinging my shoulder toward me so I could read the tattoo in times of self-doubt. Yes, I'd look a bit disabled as I'd hunch my shoulder up and rotate it towards my chest to read it more clearly, the hunched shoulder would be a small price to pay for affirmation: "There is no right way."

I love that! No more mea culpa. No more sorry. No more hung head… no more heavy wooden cross of guilt eating into my shoulder.

How liberating to know that my mis-steps were OK… maybe even acceptable. I am, after all, human. "To err is human; to forgive is Divine."

Those 3 a.m. night terrors… that Goya thing of a sleepless man beset by a leering monster… that cracked celluloid film. The sound has crackles and the picture has faded, but the film is caught in an endless loop warped by time. Round and round it goes as it plays and replays all the mis-steps I have taken.

It's a purgatory thing. I'm in sackcloth, and my feet are blistered from walking on a bed of hot coals. And as I walk, a disembodied voice whispers…

"Remember when you failed your best friend Pam? Remember when you failed your wayward child? Remember when you failed your mother?"

The failures keep coming and only dawn and the smell of coffee brings the light which sends the trolls underground.

Will I come to praise these pin pricks and growing self-awareness? I think I will.

Tomorrow I'm going to get that tattoo.

What do you do over and over again?

We're here…listening…

I was ten years old when I took swimming lessons for the first and last time. I learned to dog paddle and hold my breath underwater. These were big accomplishments for me then, but I've never gone any further with my swimming skills.

I still swim like a 10-year-old who's had just a handful of swimming lessons. Mostly splashing, refusing to open my eyes underwater.

We grew up on a lake, a little reservoir on the James River. We had a speed boat and we all learned to water ski. On hot summer days, we'd find a quiet bay and drop the anchor, swim off the side in our life jackets. I loved those days on the water. But all I know about floating involves a flotation device. I have never gotten the feel for the buoyancy of my own body.

I would like to learn this skill. Or really, from what I understand, it's an unlearning of rigidity, a physical act of trust, a counter-intuitive response to lie back and be held by the vast, terrifying mystery of water -- a medium that makes up more then 90% of my body, but will kill me if it takes up that much of my lungs.

I am afraid to trust the quiver of deep water with the weight of my body.

I would like to learn this lesson before I die. I don't need to know how to snorkle or dive or pull my body through pools, scissor-kicking my legs, opening my eyes to the liquid light below. I simply would love to learn to let go and know with the wisdom of muscle and bone that I will be held.

After Penny read her piece Charlotte offered to take her to the local pool and hold her up until Penny was ready for Charlotte to let her go. What would you like help with?

Dana was the best swimmer of the three of us. Her dad used to call her a fish because she was in their pool more than she was out of it in the summer. She and Alice and I used to have tea parties at the bottom of their shallow end. We'd all take a huge breath, puff out our cheeks, and wiggle our way to the bottom, wave to one another, lift our cups to our lips, pinkies extended, then burst to the surface when our lungs couldn't stand it any longer. Then we'd do it again. We were 6, 8, 9, 11, who knows.

I was three when we moved to Merion. Alice and Dana were already on Hill Road, three doors away from one another. We lived around the corner on Cleary Road close enough that Dana and I thought we might be able to send messages to one another at night. We tried to run a pulley from my bedroom to hers using an old ball of cotton yarn my grandmother'd given me. We were going to put our notes in the tissue box we'd hung from the yarn with a paper clip, but the man next door to her wouldn't let us climb his fence to get the yarn across, so we gave up.

Dana was half Japanese. Her grandparents owned a gift shop called Osara's in Berwyn. I loved that store. It was so exotic! They had Japanese sandles, kimono sashes, and chop sticks to push through your hair. Dana's grandmother spoke Japanese, too, which was scary and thrilling at the same time.

Alice was 100% WASP. Her dad was head of Pediatrics at The University of Pennsylvania. He had a dry sense of humor, a long, bulbous nose, and a wide, open grin that makes me smile to think about now. He'd tease us and tickle us. He even let us listen to our hearts through his stethoscope. Alice's mom was the opposite. She was always reading or lecturing us about what to do and what not to do. Their house had a stairway that split at the bottom. One side led to the front hall where they had a love seat; the other went down to the den with the '60s leather seats that I thought were cool. When I think of that room, I remember the day Alice's brother Paul got his draft number for Viet Nam. He looked sick as he opened the envelope, but then a smile formed on his face. He didn't have to go. I was 12 with a huge crush on him. He was handsome and nice to me. I didn't understand any of it except his smile.

Dana's mother, Jane, thought I was a bad influence on Dana. She was the kind of mom who read her daughter's diary as well as any notes passed between Dana and me. I'd used the word 'shit' at some point and that crime followed me for years afterwards.

One summer during high school the three of us invited Mick, Teddy, and John over for lunch at my house. We made a restaurant in the basement where they could order from a menu and we could serve them. They were neighborhood friends we'd grown up with but now had crushes on. We'd climbed trees together, gone to scout meetings at the same church, and gone ice skating on the lake at the bottom of the hill we lived on. We hung white sheets in the basement to create a small room with a table in the middle. The menu had only one choice: Bacon, Lettuce, and

Tomato. Because it was my house, the cooking was left to me.

I'd never made a BLT, nor had I ever seen one made, so I did what I thought was right: I put the raw bacon strips, the lettuce, and the sliced tomato on the bread and threw the sandwiches in the oven. Maybe that's why none of them ever married us!

When was your cooking embarrassing?

*

I hear a voice or some kind of note in my head, in my ear, 'whales', and I smell the ocean, feel the liquid bracing my body, pushing and pulling, melding and softening, but mostly it's beckoning, imploring, cajoling, whispering, 'whales', there's singing now, moaning, light and dark, and I sink into those voices, those notes in my head, in my ear and I go under and it's beautiful, like swimming into forever, the sun and moon reflecting, so blue, so soft and alive, and I keep sinking down further, feeling the skin of the whales, the breath of eternity, and I'll stay here always and it's oh so lovely.

If you could swim with anyone, who would it be?

I'm not sure if I remember, really, but my fingers gripped the chain link fence and I stood there in my new bathing suit, sobbing, begging, 'please don't make me stay!'

I must have been 4, 5, 6? years old. Young, I know that. And my mom, who was afraid of the water herself and determined not to pass it along to me, had delivered me to swimming lessons at the local pool. She was sitting on the bleachers on the other side of the fence with the other mothers.

She told me this story many times when I was older, so I don't know about the vivid image of my little fingers gripping the chain link fence and my tears part, but I do remember I was scared to put my face in the water and to do the proper breathing. And diving? Oh how I wished I could be one of the kids who stood up straight and sliced into the water, in perfect form, with arms upstretched and a little lift-off bounce on their toes before diving. I tended to bend my knees and plop in, sometimes with a belly splash. And I always wanted to hold my nose too, which really wrecked my form.

Later, at the lake, Daddy gave me a bribe, a promise, one that meant a lot to me. "I'll give you a transistor radio if you learn to swim, if you pass intermediate level."

That summer, on the dock and in the water, splashing with my cousins, I learned enough to swim out to him and after that, we went to buy my coveted radio together.

I've never been a smooth, strong swimmer, but I lost my fear of the water that summer and have since enjoyed being buoyant enough. If I were shipwrecked in strong waves in the middle of an ocean, a doggie paddle, treading water and knowing how to float might – might – save me.

But that transistor ushered in a new era for me for sure. At bedtime, when I was supposed to be sleeping, I kept it under my pillow and at a low volume and I dialed in to the Detroit radio stations across the sound waves of Lake Erie and Ohio. Motown, Top 40, Chi-Lites, Marvin Gaye and Tammy Terrell … I was swimming in musical pleasure long after lights out every night. I had learned to swim and got all new music as my reward.

When I was in first grade, I traded a bunch of my sister's Barbie Doll clothes for a friend's transistor? What did you trade that wasn't yours to give away?

Black Prince Tomatoes, Black Bread, Basil, and Butter

Longer Nights

Take Care

remember us?

This house has most of its windows facing south, and being here, I am more aware of the light than any other place I've lived. In the heart of winter, the sun rises directly through the one east window, in the kitchen, then hangs so low in the sky all day, shining in, that the furnace shuts off at 9 a.m. and doesn't come back on until the sun drops behind mountains close to 5 p.m.

In summer, that same sun rises high and the roof shades all but a few direct rays in the early morning and middle evening, when the heat is already cut out of the day here at 8000 feet above sea level.

It is the sun I most follow, taking its progress like a long, rambling story. When it goes down, the night is almost like nodding off while watching a movie. The longer darkness tells a story, too, I suppose, but I only catch it in snatches, disjointed. A plot I cannot entirely piece together.

"I love the dark hours of my being," Rilke wrote in one of his love poems to God. A curious line. Because all the unknowns, the mysteries, lay in the dark hours. The womb. The place of waiting. The slow, creeping growth.

What do you do when you first wake up? What do you do late at night?

I helped buy the tomato plants but I didn't put them in the pots. Not that time nor did I plant the kale or the cucumbers or the squash. I helped pick the strawberries because I loved them so. Finding them under the green leaves felt like finding a prize. They reminded me of summers in Iowa, picking strawberries with my mother, just the two of us, me following her lead.

"Not the white ones or the pink ones. Only the red. See there? Careful…"

Mom was at peace in the strawberry patch. In my mind it was a giant triangle and she was at the center, stooped, lost in thought, content, not thinking of suicide, not yelling at my father.

If I was good, really good, I could keep that rope off her neck. I could convince her not to drive her car off of the bridge. I could prove to her I was worth staying around for. But I didn't. I couldn't. I quit trying, but I never accepted that I was powerless to change her trajectory.

What was your mother thinking? How would she answer that question?

Sam Williams had skin as dark and creamy as I'd ever seen. What I remember better, though, was the quiet way he spoke and the low, slow way he walked. Everything about him was slow except his mind. His graceful hands, his gentle eyes – both calm. He had the whitest, shyest smile. He studied Political Science, hoping to go to law school, hoping even more to change the world.

For graduation he gave me an inscribed copy of Chaucer's *Canterbury Tales*. Hardcover. He'd found it an antique store somewhere. Clearly he had more confidence in my literary aptitude than I did. I could never follow, nor was I interested in reading Old English, or any of the classics an English Literature Major was meant to love. What I appreciated was the thought behind the book. No one had ever given me a gift that suggested I had a mind.

But the gift was disturbing too. It was too much, too intimate. Sam was not my boyfriend, although the inscription confirmed that he wished otherwise. What he wrote was benign. It was the length and the thoughtfulness. We were young after all. I can still see his handwriting: careful, even, smooth, with words well considered. I wonder if I broke his heart without knowing.

We were seniors when he asked me to go to his hometown on a Saturday. Manhattan. He was one of the lucky ones who had a car. Driving from Pennsylvania east to the city with my blackest friend was more than a simple car ride. I had never been to New York alone with a friend. I had never left campus in a friend's car to do anything other than get French Fries at MacDonald's down the hill. Even that was rare. This trip was scarier. Farther away. Riskier and dangerous in some brain-washed sort of way - as though a person silly enough to travel into the great city got what they asked for.

Sam's car was big. A sedan, American of course, with a long front seat and a vast windshield. We left campus in time to watch the sunrise on Route 22 through New Jersey's horse country. I can remember the colors of the sky even now although I'd forgotten we'd left so early in the day. The memory of pinks and oranges as we went east tells me the one thing I wouldn't have remembered otherwise: I spent the whole day with Sam.

Funny how a single detail gives me enough to remember so much more.

Sam took me to Greenwich Village. We walked and walked, ate a meal somewhere. We must have, but what I remember was my constant awareness of his blackness and my whiteness. I could feel other people's eyes on us even when they weren't looking. I remember Stuart's hand reaching for mine at an intersection. Aware, too, of my need to let go of his hand on the other side of the street.

I wasn't his girlfriend. I needed others to know. I couldn't be. I didn't love him in that way. That was part of the struggle.

What gift did you receive that meant more than you were ready for?

As Charlotte read her response to the prompt **Black Prince Tomatoes, Black Bread, Basil, and Butter** *she realized her memory must have been wrong. There was no way she and Sam would have left campus early enough to see the sun rise. It must have been the sun setting on their way home that she saw.*

Does it matter?

Have you ever described something incorrectly and decided to let it go rather than correct yourself?

see us?

I applied for the job because it was work I enjoyed, for an organization I believed in and a boss I liked. Also, I needed the paycheck. I had been in Minneapolis for eight months and was surviving hand-to-mouth on freelance jobs. I had applied for anything I could find -- telemarketing, waitressing, dog-walking, tutoring -- and hardly got a call back. In a university town, I was over-qualified.

So when the associate pastor at the church where Jack was working needed a new admin assistant, I was hopeful I might be a good fit. I contacted Tim. He invited me in for an interview. Then he offered me the part time job.

Church staffs are little like sausage factories. They turn out some tasty products, but the process in the back room can be nasty. Church is all about spiritual life in the context of community. And this community had been broken down by some tough stuff, most of which they'd done to each other. Jack had been called in as a specialist interim pastor. And the church staff was part of the puzzle that needed some help.

I had worked on a church staff with Jack before, in Wisconsin. It is where I'd met him. It is where, in fact, I had fallen in love with him. My first marriage was unraveling at that time. His first marriage had been on secret life-support for years. That is a whole story for another time.

But when Jack came to Minneapolis, the congregation knew he was going through a divorce. When I moved to town and started to show up at church, people started to talk.

People started to talk to each other, of course. Only one or two brave souls talked directly to us. Or rather, they talked to Jack. I heard nothing. But I saw everyone. I saw everyone greet me for the first time with that wide open generous midwestern hospitality. I saw bright and articulate church leaders meet me for the first time, have sincere conversations with me, invite me to participate in their community in very specific ways. And then, I could see when the rumor had gotten to them. They stopped making eye contact. They found ways to avoid me. Their conversations would go silent when I walked into a room.

I haven't thought about this painful period for almost two years.

When did you take a job that led you somewhere you didn't think you could go? When have you been talked about behind your back? What did you do to cause it? What didn't you do to cause it?

Selective hearing. Despite the fact that I am making an effort to get out and about… to reintegrate myself in the community, I see everyone and hear nothing.

After walking the Camino de Santiago, I came home… if not transformed… I came home in a bubble of goodwill and serenity. My first act was to resign from the community boards on which I served. I did not want to be tied down, and I did not want to expose myself to toxic conflict.

The five-week pilgrimage across Northern Spain taxed my body, but I thrilled to the spaciousness that comes with walking, reflection, and landscape. Most of all, awash in the friendliness of other pilgrims, each on a quest for inner peace, my heart expanded. Metaphorically I felt a mother's embrace in the warmth of strangers who did not share my language or culture. Politics never came up.

What I have found after my return is that it has been difficult to maintain the Zen-like equanimity I gained. Removing myself from local, state, national and international political dissention has been hard. I try to limit my in-take of national and international news. And yet, lying near a nest of wasps or a hill of ants, you are apprehensive – always waiting to be under attack.

I have also found that my listening skills have deteriorated. I think that I am more and more selective about what I make an effort to remember. I can be in a casual conversation, and I am aware of smiling, nodding, and questioning, but a week later… sometimes days later, I can't remember the details of the conversation.

Obviously, I am not living in-the-moment; rather, I am living in the past. I float in a bubble – afraid that it will break.

Where did you come back from that left you lost in your own life?

Summer Camp

'Summer' is a beautiful word. It conjures up thoughts of vacation, camp, Lake Winnepesaukee, skinny dipping whenever possible, the Moompah – my grandfather's double engine Chris Craft Cruiser that we were allowed to ski behind once a summer, a boat that made a dangerous wake behind it, a wake so big it was thrilling to cross it, jump over it, leap off of it, always with the possibility of a painful fall if I didn't land just right. And sometimes I'd slalom, just like mom. Right leg solidly in the rubber foot cup as I pulled the left foot away from its ski, leaving it near the dock as Moompah zoomed by, everyone on land screaming with enthusiasm, Moompah with his hat, his pipe, his Aqua Velvet, smiling because this was one special day. The left ski fell off as my loose foot slipped into the rubber cup in the back of the right ski. Lean into the back foot, slice the water, watch the wake, gather courage and go – go fast across the hill of water, landing, bent knees, bent elbows to absorb the shock. Crouch. Let the boat pull me across the second wake landing on the far side, the rough water of the harbor to navigate now. Around and around Moompah would drive until we were back at the dock. I'd let go, sink into the lake as the boat turned around to pick up the next eager skier.

Mom could slalom off the dock. Mom can do anything. I didn't think about it then. She was my mom. Whatever mom did was what all mothers did: field hockey into her 50s, slalom skiing until 1985 when they sold the boat, the house, and all the history none of us could afford to hold onto. Tennis still at 86. Voting Chairperson in her town, 16 hours a day at least once a year on election day. Physics teacher – her decision to start over after 20+ years of professional motherhood.

Mom.

What will life be like without you?

I don't lean on you in every day life. I don't call you with my problems (although you always know when I need you, you hear the quiver in my voice, you always know everything before I do). I don't do things with you – shopping or gardening or driving you to the doctor. I don't go to the grocery store for you or take you to see

your friends. You've never needed or wanted any of that. But knowing you're there, knowing I have my mom, that there's you out there, caring, watching, loving me no matter what. I've relied on that. I've needed that. What will happen to me when I don't have that anymore?

for my mom

tell us about your mother

Scrambled Eggs

Midway on Life's Journey

Tell me what you saw

Whenever I see the words 'scrambled eggs' I think of the song "Yesterday." Supposedly the Beatles sang the words "scrambled eggs" instead of "yesterday" until they wrote the final lyric. I also think of my grandparents' kitchen in New Hampshire. Every morning someone cooked scrambled eggs and bacon. The whole house smelled like breakfast and I remember how happy I was there.

What's the first thing that comes to mind when you think of your grandparents?

I loved my grandmother's scrambled eggs. Mamaw made them in bacon grease. She invited me into them with her Southern accent: "Baby? Ya'll want some breakfast? Some scrambled eggs? Bacon?" I always said 'yes.'

I can still smell Mamaw's house, how when you came in the back door you walked into a laundry room that smelled of Tide laundry detergent. A clothesline strung across it, one end to the other, the room thick with warm air from the dryer and that soapy smell.

I miss my grandmother. She started to go downhill while I was in college. I went to see her with my mother—missing days of class and taking the B instead of the A because it was worth it to see her. She died in 1989, four years after I graduated, just a couple months after my son was born. He wore a little tuxedo sleeper to her funeral. I also bought him an orange sleeper with a jack-o-lantern on the tummy because she was buried around Halloween.

My grandmothers' ankles were as wide as her calves, the tops of her feet swollen and pushing out of her shoes. She always wore dresses and stockings. I loved her little laugh—more of a "tee hee" that floated up than a boisterous laugh that filled the room. She was married to a sad, dark man—my grandfather, who I called "Papaw." When I was little he tickled me inside my panties when my mom and grandmother weren't around. I laughed, but I knew I shouldn't. I was 4, maybe. I'd sit on his lap and he tickled me all over, under my armpits, down my belly, and then his hand slipped into my panties. It's the only time I really saw him smile or heard him laugh. Mostly when we visited he said little and read or talked to my mother.

I always wondered if he molested my mother, if he were the reason she drank. I never told her he tickled me like that. I didn't want to trouble her and I didn't know how to ask if anything like that happened to her when she was a child.

My grandfather loved to read. In his attic were boxes of books about a cartoon character named Pogo. I liked to look at those books, which smelled musty from being up in the attic for so long. I liked that I knew some of the words.

In my grandparents' bathroom, my sisters and I took baths together, two at a time. We loved to look through the glass shower doors, which were opaque and made our eyes look blurry. That made us laugh.

My grandparents' home was tiny and brick and in Memphis, Tennessee. I loved to visit them because spring had already come to their yard and was still a good couple of weeks away in Iowa. We'd load up the station wagon with all of us—eight if Dad went, too. Between the suitcases and kids and pillows and blankets, I don't know how my parents could see to drive.

I loved those trips. I loved my Mamaw and her scrambled eggs.

What did you call your grandma? What did she wear? How 'bout your other grandma? Did they cook anything special for you? Something you didn't like but they made you eat?

*

Tonight I pulled up an address on Google Maps and I'll tell you what I saw. I saw my old house. The photo was taken in January 2015.

Now I'm trying to recall what I was doing during that time. I look at the picture again and imagine that I might be inside my living room having lunch or maybe I'm in the back working in the office. The living room window is open about six inches and all the other windows are closed so it must be cool outside.

Looking at this picture of my home is like looking at a picture of a family member. My house took care of me and provided safety and shelter for 15 years. I loved coming home. I look at this picture and think of happy memories. Little did I know then that I was about to go through the most turbulent time of my life. At the time, I didn't know that Brian and I would sell that house six months later, that I would leave my hometown and my husband behind.

When I look at that house I see happiness, contentment, joy, laughter, family, friends and comfort. I see all the love we put into the house. I remember the extensive renovations. I remember Brian taking every window out, sanding them down and painting them, and then repairing the ropes on each one so they would go up and down smoothly. I remember designing the front iron gate, picking out the tiles around the door and the paint colors. I remember the care he took in choosing every plant, tree and flower in our yard. From the little brass bell at the front door to the verde green mailbox, to the herringbone pattern in the old Chicago brick walkway, we chose every detail. I miss that house. I miss my life. I would give anything to go back in time and live one more day – as a happy couple – in that house.

That house represents my marriage and the life my husband and I built together, from scratch, and the love we shared with one another.

What happened to that man? Why can't I have him back? Why was he taken from me? Everything was taken from me. Now all I have is a photograph and my memories.

What do you have left?

The sun shining bright and the wind chimes on the front porch moving this way and that with the wind. That same wind that swirled around the house and picked up and dropped off shingle after shingle in the front and back yards. I'll tell you what I saw (and heard) on the road that passes in front of the house—a car, just one, towing a trailer-sized horse carrier only its emptiness rattled around inside and left a hollowness behind, right there on the road.

Did I tell you I saw the effects of silence on my city ears? I didn't feel it though I guess that seems like the way it should have been. I saw it happen over the past two years as the grass grew up. The wind through the blades would tickle my eardrums a little in spring and rise to a thumping sound as the blades seemed to fill out and the wind had to wind around and through. I could see the 'o's' as the wind touched the blades in the full heat of summer and 'ee's' as it thinned in the fall.

I'll tell you what I saw that day, that last day before the neighbor moved in. In the distance, across the pond, I watched the ducks settle within it, saw with my mind's eye the fluttering of their webbed feet holding them atop the water. They floated in rhythm with the pearlescent green algae one just as pretty as the other. There in the pond I saw unison, the way nature sits with itself and finds a peaceful moment.

When do you remember hearing silence?

What I first see is the long, green tunnel of the Appalachian Trail, a tangle of fecund growth. Over growth and under. Dense. Intimate or maybe cloying in a way the wide western landscape is not.

What I saw first, and see next, is distance. Wide, hard space almost impossible to compass with the unaccustomed imagination. Not just the green squares of the midwest, its gently rolling ground marked off by country roads, farm houses, shelter belts of trees and water towers over high school football fields. But something all together bigger.

Rocks catching in clouds. Jagged runs of scree over cliffs. Miles of exposure. Dusty air. Dry ground. A wilderness of oppressive distance instead of a wilderness of suffocating tangle.

What am I midway across? And what do I see from here? It would take a book to tell that, including the landscapes, but also the smaller, ordinary things in front of me, seen clearly, almost fresh.

For instance, all my life I have eaten scrambled eggs, but there is enormous variety in that. My mother's early eggs — dry and crumbly. Then the kind they served at camp — watery and tasteless. But how rich they can be, cooked in too much butter and not over-done. Or the technique, apparently ancient, from culinary France: whisking eggs over a double-boiler with with butter! Hard to believe the tender, custardy result has anything at all to do with summer camp variety I ate at Camp Okaboji.

So here is what I see I'm seeing — here at the midway point to something: that trees have endless moods and big rocks that can kill you just as easily as you can carry a small one in your pocket. That scrambled eggs can make you afraid to swallow. Or they can slip down your throat like pudding.

What I see is that even if the view never changes for the next half of life, there will never be an end to seeing as long as I am willing to look.

What did you see in the distance? What was under your feet?

These pages are for notes, doodles, ideas, overflow, whatever you need. Fill 'em up!

write

write

write

write

When I respond to prompts, I almost always write in first person. It's personal and memoir-esque. I'm guessing you might respond to prompts that way too. Here are some issues that many memoirists struggle with:

Don't let forgetting the facts keep you from writing the truth. None of us remember verbatim the irritating conversation we had with our mom when we got home late from the prom. The dialogue you re-create is meant to give the reader the essence of your conversation: mom's exasperation the way she would have expressed it, your snippy response the way you would have mumbled it.

Often the truth as we see it is different from the truth as our siblings or parents sees it. This can keep you from writing, too. The word 'memoir' comes from the same Latin root ('*memoria*') as 'memory.' Needless to say, our memories are inherently flawed. If I tell a story about how the family dog ate the couch when we were kids, it's going to be different than my brother's account of the same dog and couch. Both versions are true. Write yours. Let your brother write his.

Recently I had to edit a story I'd written that involved something my husband did many, many years ago and which eventually involved me. I wrestled with how to be sure I didn't trespass on his privacy. I weighed it and weighed it. In the end, I scrapped the story. My sharing it wasn't worth the worry of wondering if I'd trespassed, and I didn't want to give him the power to decide for me. It was a nice story too, painted him in a very good light, but in the end it was his story to tell, not mine. I wrote another story instead. The important thing is to write the story, then decide if you want to share it or not.

If you're thinking about writing a book you're probably asking yourself, *where do I start? How do I end?* The best advice I ever got from another writer was "start in the middle." Our memories aren't chronological so why would our stories have to be? Start somewhere. Start with the story that you feel like writing today. Finish it tomorrow or the next day then write another story that you feel like writing. Worry about how it will all fit together when you don't have any more stories to tell. When you finally put it all together, that'll probably be your first draft. Then get ready for your second, your third, and your fourth. When I was writing *The Present Giver*, I made a list of all the stories I knew I'd eventually want to tell. On a day when I couldn't think of anything to write, I looked at my list and wrote the story that jumped out at me that day. It worked.

Whether you're self-publishing or presenting your work to an agent or publisher, ask trusted readers to take a look before you submit. Don't ask your mom, your spouse, or your best friend. Often these people have too much power over your decision-making. Ask writers you admire who don't know you well, or regular people who read a lot and don't know you well. See what comments they offer. See if multiple readers make the same comments. Be careful, though. They may not be right. But if a number of people say the same thing you might want to reevaluate. Ultimately, though, you're the judge of what's working or not. Trust thyself.

Before you start a project, be clear about what you want to write and why. Write it down and remember your reasons as you write. If you're writing to inspire others to climb the Himalayas like you did, make your stories inspiring. Don't skip the scary parts, or the parts where you doubted yourself. If you're writing the same book for climbers who have already done extreme climbs, maybe you include more technical details, or the special supplies the reader will need. One book is meant to inspire, the other is meant to educate. Different books. Different innards. If you know why you're writing something it'll help you decide what to keep and what to discard.

Find a way to make writing something you look forward to rather that a chore you have to do.

Have fun with it.

Love, Bar

Bar Scott leads writing workshops in Colorado and New York.
She also coaches writers and songwriters in person, by phone, and via skype.
She often likes the results when she writes or hums something quickly and without much time to think.

Published writing includes her memoir, *The Present Giver (ALM Books , 2011)*
"Grace" from *Stories of Music, Volume One* (Timbre Press, 2015)
and "Valentine" from *Three Minus One*, (SheWritesPress, 2014)
She has recorded seven albums of original words and music, and has published over 70 songs.

For more information visit www.barscott.com, or email her at bar@barscott.com

If your writing group would like multiple copies of this or any of Bar's other books or CDs,
contact ALM Books for a discount.

Send Bar an email if you want to hear about future
Lone Writer's Writing Club workbooks

Thank you!

Recommended Reading:

Art and Fear, Ted Orland and David Bayles

What it Is, Lynda Barry

If You Want to Write, Brenda Ueland,

Thinking About Memoir, Abigail Thomas,

On Writing, Stephen King,

"Place" an essay by Dorothy Allison

The Lone Writer's Writing Club, Volume 1,
Published by ALM Books
POB 576, Westcliffe, CO 81252 USA   p:719 371 0228

Bar Scott, Editor and organizer

Cover Design: Erin Papa at The Turning Mill, Palenville, NY.
(With help from someone who always makes me smile, Lucy Swenson)

Photo of Bar ©J.E. Ward, 2016

Made in the USA
Las Vegas, NV
06 March 2023

68639539R00063